本书为2022年度《国际中文教育中文水平等级标准》教学资源建设项目
"对标《等级标准》的多模态中英对照四川文化读物建设研究"成果；
四川大学创新火花项目库"城镇化进程中多民族社区语言景观研究"
（项目号：2018hhs-09）阶段性成果

第二眼看四川

向世界讲述四川故事

李韵 于婧 著

·汉英对照·

Second Glance At Sichuan

Telling Sichuan Stories To The World

图书在版编目（CIP）数据

第二眼看四川：向世界讲述四川故事：汉英对照 / 李韵，于婧著. -- 成都：四川大学出版社，2025.8.
ISBN 978-7-5690-7454-3

Ⅰ．K871.34；G127.71

中国国家版本馆 CIP 数据核字第 2025WF8133 号

书　　　名：	第二眼看四川：向世界讲述四川故事
	Di-er Yan Kan Sichuan: Xiang Shijie Jiangshu Sichuan Gushi
著　　　者：	李　韵　于　婧
出　版　人：	侯宏虹
总　策　划：	张宏辉
选题策划：	周　洁
责任编辑：	周　洁
责任校对：	敬雁飞
装帧设计：	叶　茂
责任印制：	李金兰
出版发行：	四川大学出版社有限责任公司
地　　　址：	成都市一环路南一段 24 号（610065）
电　　　话：	（028）85408311（发行部）、85400276（总编室）
电子邮箱：	scupress@vip.163.com
网　　　址：	https://press.scu.edu.cn
印前制作：	成都墨之创文化传播有限公司
印刷装订：	四川五洲彩印有限责任公司
成品尺寸：	155mm×235mm
印　　　张：	15.25
插　　　页：	1
字　　　数：	221 千字
版　　　次：	2025 年 8 月 第 1 版
印　　　次：	2025 年 8 月 第 1 次印刷
定　　　价：	88.00 元

本社图书如有印装质量问题，请联系发行部调换

版权所有 ◆ 侵权必究

扫码获取数字资源

四川大学出版社
微信公众号

前言

一、本书目标

在跨文化传播中,"第一眼"看四川看的是神奇九寨、麻辣川菜、国宝熊猫等文化符号,而"第二眼"要看的则是这些文化符号背后的四川故事与精神。故本书以"第二眼看四川"为名,期待和读者一道在阅读中品味四川故事与精神,习得中文。

二、本书特色

作为一本四川文化读物,本书特色如下:

一是阅读中学中文:本书文本难度与语言点讲解对应《国际中文教育中文水平等级标准》(以下简称《等级标准》)的"中等"指标,在文化内容创作与练习设计方面的读者定位为青少年及成人;

二是形式上应需求:本书出版融合纸质书、数字书与有声资源,适应信息时代"时时可学、处处能学"的阅读需求;

三是中英文相对照:本书以中英双语讲述"四川故事",既可作为中文学习者的自学材料、国内外高校的四川文化课教材,同时还可作为四川文化对外传播读本,为全球各界人士理解四川提供窗口。

三、内容构成

全书正文共分为8篇,每篇一个主题,包括4篇短文。每一课构成如下:

短文阅读　《等级标准》对"中等"水平等级的描述为：理解多种主题的一般语言材料，能够就较为复杂的话题进行基本的成段表达，基本了解中国文化知识等。本书参照这一描述，以《等级标准》中 1~6 级的语言量化指标为依据编写短文。

语言点例释　每课短文后的"语言点例释"栏目，对文中出现的 1~2 个重要词语或结构予以例释并延伸。这些重要语言点均为《等级标准》中 4~7 级的新增词语或结构，习得难度较大。

延伸阅读　有的短文后还设有"延伸阅读"栏目，对文中出现的文化典故、名人名言等进行拓展介绍。

读后思考　每课短文后均设有"读后思考"栏目，引导读者对短文大意进行总结，或是对文中细节进行分析。

亲身体验　除了对短文本身的理解考察，每课短文后的"亲身体验"栏目设计有体验活动、小组讨论等练习题目，体现了"用中学"的教育理念，旨在带领读者进行中外文化比较与跨文化交际，透过现象理解中国精神。

四、中文学习建议

我们建议中文学习者依照以下步骤使用本书：

第一步：阅读短文。在阅读时应以汉语文本为主、英语文本为辅，尽量在完成"读后思考"后再利用英语文本对学习成果进行检验，以达成扩大词汇量、巩固语法学习与提高中文阅读能力的目标。

第二步：温故知新。在阅读后，运用文后"语言点例释"进行语言点复习与学习。

第三步：拓展学习。以"亲身体验"为线索，在四川本地或网络中寻找相关资源，进行拓展阅读与文化体验。

第四步：泛在学习。除了阅读纸质书，充分利用本书电子版和中文部分的音频材料进行自主学习，综合训练汉语听、说、读、写的能力。

Second Glance at Sichuan: Telling Sichuan Stories to the World

Preface

In cross-cultural communication, the first impression of Sichuan includes the magical Jiuzhaigou National Park, spicy Sichuan cuisine, giant panda and other cultural symbols. However, the "second glance" aims to explore the Sichuan stories and spirit behind these cultural symbols. Therefore, this book is titled "Second Glance at Sichuan", hoping to guide readers in savoring Sichuan and learning Chinese through reading.

As a cultural publication about Sichuan, this book possesses the following characteristics:

(1) Learning Chinese through Reading: The text difficulty and language point explanations in this book correspond to the "Intermediate" level of the *Chinese Proficiency Standards for International Chinese Language Education* (hereinafter referred to briefly as *The Standards*), targeting teenagers and adults in terms of cultural content creation and exercise design.

(2) Form to Meet Needs: The publication of this book integrates

print, digital, and audio resources, catering to the reading demands of the information age where learning is possible anytime and anywhere.

(3) Chinese-English Bilingual: The book narrates "Sichuan Stories" in both Chinese and English, serving as self-study material for Chinese learners, a textbook on Sichuan culture for higher education at home and abroad, as well as a reading resource for the external dissemination of Sichuan culture, offering a window for people worldwide to understand Sichuan.

3. Content Composition

The text of the book is divided into 8 chapters, each of which is a theme with 4 units. Each unit is structured as follows:

Text Reading: According to *The Standards*, the description of the "Intermediate" level includes the ability to understand general language materials on various topics, the capability to express basic paragraphs on relatively complex topics, and a basic understanding of Chinese cultural knowledge. Following this description, the text of this book is written based on the language quantification indicators of levels 1-6 in *The Standards*.

Notes: This section following each text provides explanations and extensions for 1-2 important words or grammatical patterns that appear in the text. These important language points are newly added words or patterns at levels 4-7 in *The Standards* and may pose a higher level of

difficulty in acquisition.

Extensive Reading: Some units are accompanied by an "Extensive Reading" section, which expands on cultural allusions, famous quotes, and other elements mentioned in the text.

Questions: This section guides readers to summarize the main ideas of the text or analyze the details within by answering questions.

Experience: In addition to assessing comprehension of the text itself, the "Experience" section includes activities and group discussions to facilitate a hands-on approach and encourage readers to engage in cross-cultural communication and understanding of Chinese spirit through comparative analysis.

4. Suggestions for Chinese Learning

We recommend Chinese learners to follow these steps when using this book:

Step 1: Text Reading. Focus on the Chinese text while using the English text as a supplement. Try to test your understanding by completing the "Questions" section in Chinese before checking your results with the English translation to expand your vocabulary, reinforce grammar learning, and improve Chinese reading skills.

Step 2: Review and Learn. After reading, utilize the "Notes" section for language point review and learning.

Step 3: Expand Learning. Use the "Experience" section as a guide to explore related resources in Sichuan locally or online for extended

reading and cultural experiences.

Step 4: Ubiquitous Learning. In addition to reading the physical book, make full use of the electronic version and audio materials in Chinese for independent study, integrating training in Chinese listening, speaking, reading, and writing abilities.

目录

一、概况篇 1
（一）四川在哪儿？ 2
（二）四川人是谁？ 7
（三）四川怎么样？ 15
（四）四川话啥样？ 22

二、自然篇 29
（一）童话世界——九寨沟自然保护区 30
（二）"滚滚"的家——卧龙自然保护区 38
（三）天空跑道——稻城亚丁 46
（四）守卫长江——诺水河水生动物自然保护区 52

三、民族篇 61
（一）云朵上的民族——羌族 62
（二）大山的桃花源——纳西族古寨 68
（三）燃烧的狂欢节——彝族火把节 74
（四）各民族一家亲——川西康巴文化 82

四、历史篇 89
（一）灿烂三星堆 90
（二）浪漫金沙 96
（三）传奇三国（上） 103
（四）传奇三国（下） 110

五、古迹篇　119
（一）"天府之国"的守卫——都江堰　120
（二）古代战场的见证——剑门关　126
（三）诗意生活之感动——杜甫草堂　133
（四）道教文化的代表——青羊宫　139

六、人物篇　147
（一）政治双星　148
（二）治水双星　153
（三）文学双星　158
（四）科学双星　166

七、风物篇　173
（一）一杯茶，一段时光——川茶　174
（二）一段锦，一座城市——蜀锦　181
（三）一道菜，百种味道——川菜　189
（四）一口锅，一个江湖——火锅　195

八、艺术篇　203
（一）可不只是"变脸"——川剧　204
（二）可不只是画画——绵竹年画　210
（三）可不只是唱歌——四川清音　215
（四）可不只是一种舞蹈——四川少数民族舞蹈　222

后记　229

Contents

1. **Overview**   1

    (1) Where Is Sichuan?   4

    (2) Who Are the Sichuan People?   10

    (3) How Is Sichuan?   18

    (4) What Is Sichuan Dialect?   25

2. **Nature**   29

    (1) Jiuzhaigou National Park: A Fairyland   34

    (2) Wolong Nature Reserve: Home of Giant Pandas   42

    (3) Daocheng Yading: Running Track to the Sky   49

    (4) Nuoshuihe National Nature Reserve for Rare Aquatic Animals: Protection of Yangtze River   56

3. **National Minorities**   61

    (1) Qiang Ethnic Group: People Living on the Clouds   65

    (2) Naxi Ancient Village: Peach Blossom Spring Amongst the Mountains   71

    (3) Burning Carnival: Torch Festival of Yi Ethnic Group   78

    (4) Kham Culture in Western Sichuan: All Ethnic Groups, One Happy Family   84

4. **History**   89

    (1) Glorious Sanxingdui   93

    (2) Romantic Jinsha   99

    (3) Legendary Three Kingdoms Period (Part I)   106

    (4) Legendary Three Kingdoms Period (Part II)   113

5. Historical Sites   119

    (1) Dujiangyan: Guardian of the "Land of Abundance"   123

    (2) Jianmen Pass: Witness to Ancient Battlefield   130

    (3) Du Fu Thatched Cottage: Reminder of a Poetic Life   136

    (4) Qingyang Palace: Representative of Taoism   142

6. People   147

    (1) Two Political Figures   150

    (2) Two Stars of Flood Control and Management   155

    (3) Two Literary Stars   161

    (4) Two Scientific Stars   168

7. Specialties   173

    (1) Sichuan Tea: A Cup of Tea, a Taste of Time   177

    (2) Shu Jin: A Brocade, a City   184

    (3) Sichuan Cuisine: One Dish, Countless Flavors   192

    (4) Hot Pot: One Pot, One World   198

8. Art   203

    (1) Sichuan Opera: More than Face-Changing   206

    (2) Mianzhu New Year Prints: More than Pictures   212

    (3) Sichuan Qingyin: More than Singing   218

    (4) Folk Dances of Ethnic Minorities in Sichuan: More than Dancing   224

Postscript   230

一、概况篇

四川在哪儿？住着什么人？生活怎么样？四川人还讲一种特别可爱的方言？本篇用四篇短文为你回答这四个问题，讲述四川概况。

1. Overview

Where is Sichuan? Who lives there? What about the life and the very lovely dialect there? In this article, four short sections answer these questions to help you get to know Sichuan.

第二眼看四川：
向世界讲述四川故事
Second Glance at Sichuan: Telling Sichuan Stories to the World

（一）四川在哪儿？

四川省，简称"川"或"蜀"，在中国的西南地区。从地图上我们可以看到，四川省在中国的"肚子"的位置，说得书面一点儿，就是在中国的"腹地"。四川省的东边连接重庆，南边连接云南、贵州，西边连接西藏，北边和陕西、甘肃、青海是邻居。可以说，四川在中国西部的中心位置。正是因为这样的地理位置，四川的交通承担着联系周边地区的重要责任，因此不论是航空、铁路，还是公路、水路建设，四川都处于全国领先水平。四川的省会成都，在 2020 年拥有了第二个大型国际机场——成都天府国际机场。这个机场是"国家级国际航空枢纽""丝绸之路经济带中等级最高的航空港"，负责从成都出发的全部国际航线。现在大家来四川旅行、学习或工作都非常方便。

四川省总面积 48.6 万平方千米，是中国面积第五大省。这个面积到底有多大呢？我们可以把四川省拿来和其他城市或者国家的面积比比看：四川省的面积相当于 29.62 个北京市，或者相当于整个日本面积的 1.29 倍。这样我们就能发现，四川省的面积非常广大。在这样广大的一片土地上，地貌种类非常复杂。我们可以看看地图，东部是四川盆地，西部是川西高原，和青藏高原相连接。首先我们来看盆地部分。你以前学过"盆地"这个词吗？这个词很形象，"盆"是水盆的意思。请想象一下，这个地区就好像是一个水盆，四周高，中间低。然后我们再来看川西高原，"高原"的"高"是指海拔很高。从川西高原再往西就是青藏高原了，是全世界海拔最高的地方。

地貌不同，气候就多样。四川盆地的气候全年温暖潮湿，春、夏、秋、冬四个季节分明；而川西高原的气候随着海拔升高，变

化很大,整体而言比较湿冷,只有干季和湿季两种。所以,在四川有一个常见的现象:到了夏天,很多住在四川东部的人会去西部,为的是躲开夏天的炎热;到了冬天,很多住在四川西部的人又会来四川东部,为的是躲开冬季的寒冷。这样来来往往,开车3个小时左右,就能实现"换一个季节"!

因为有这么丰富的气候、地貌变化,四川是一个很适合旅游的地方。在四川,我们可以看到繁华的都市、美丽的自然风景、独具特色的高原风光等。无论你偏爱哪种风景,到四川都绝对不会失望。

语言点例释

1. 四川的交通承担着联系周边地区的重要责任。

"承担"是一个动词,常见的搭配有"~责任、义务、任务、工作"。例如"每个人都应该承担起保护环境的义务"。

2. 到了夏天,很多住在四川东部的人会去西部,为的是躲开夏天的炎热;到了冬天,很多住在四川西部的人又会来四川东部,为的是躲开冬季的寒冷。

"……,为的是……"可以用来表示目的。例如"我把车停在外面,为的是走的时候方便"。这个句子中,"把车停在外面"的目的是"走的时候方便"。

延伸阅读

"四川"名字的由来

北宋时,"路"大概相当于今天的"省"。那时的政府将四川盆地一带称为川峡路。为了加强管理,又把川峡路分为益州路、梓州路、利州路和夔州路,合称为"川峡四路"或"四川路",后来简称"四川"。

读后思考

1. 四川在中国哪个部分?省会是哪个城市?

2. 四川的地貌主要可以分为哪两个部分?

第二眼看四川：
向世界讲述四川故事
Second Glance at Sichuan: Telling Sichuan Stories to the World

🌀 亲身体验 🌀

你去过四川哪些地方？或者你想去哪些地方？这些地方有什么特点？最吸引你的是什么？

你去过，或者想去的地方	
为什么想去这些地方	
这些地方的特色	

(1) Where Is Sichuan?

Sichuan province, also called "Chuan" or "Shu" for short, lies in southwest China. As the map indicates, Sichuan province is located in the "belly" regions of China, or to put in more formally, it is in the "hinterland" ["腹地 (fùdì)" in Chinese] of China. Sichuan is bounded by Chongqing in the east, Xizang in the west, Yunnan and Guizhou in the south, and Shaanxi, Gansu as well as Qinghai in the north. Sichuan is arguably the regional center of west China. Because of such a superior geographic location, it does undertake an important role in connecting the regions nearby. Therefore, no matter in the fields of aviation transportation, railway transportation, or in the construction of highways and waterways, Sichuan has always remained at the leading domestic level. In 2020, Chengdu, the capital city of Sichuan, has seen the completion of its second major international airport—Chengdu Tianfu International Airport. This airport, as a national-level "International Aviation Hub" and one of the highest-ranking airports on the Silk Road Economic Belt, handles all the international flights departing from Chengdu. It is now truly wonderful and convenient for people to visit Sichuan, as well as study and work in there.

Sichuan, with the total area of 486,000 square kilometers, ranks the fifth largest province in China. Then how big exactly is the area? Compared with other cities or counties, its area equals 29.62 times that of Beijing, or 1.29 times that of Japan. Such a vast land boasts complex and diverse landforms. As it shows in the map, in the east is the Sichuan Basin, and in the west is the Western Sichuan Plateau, adjoining the Qinghai-Xizang Plateau. Have you ever heard "盆地 (péndì)" before? It is a very vivid expression: "盆 (pén)" literally means "basin" in Chinese. That's because the region is just like a basin with a high surrounding and a lower center. The Western Sichuan Plateau is called "川西高原 (Chuānxī Gāoyuán)" in Chinese. The character "高 (gāo)" means high altitude. Moving further west from the Western Sichuan Plateau is the Qinghai-Xizang Plateau, the highest plateau in the world.

Diverse landforms bring various climates. Overall, the climate of the Sichuan Basin is warm and humid all year round, with four distinctive seasons; while the climate of the Western Sichuan Plateau varies significantly with the rise of altitude, generally speaking, it's colder and wetter, with a dry season and a wet season. Thus, it's really common in Sichuan to see people who live in the eastern regions spending their summer in the west in order to drive off the heat; on the contrary, people living in the western part of Sichuan go to the eastern Sichuan in winter to escape the fierce coldness. About a three-hour drive can make the seasons change. How amazing!

Thanks to the variety of climates and landforms, Sichuan is a great destination for traveling. In Sichuan, people can experience prosperous

cities, beautiful scenic views as well as unique landscapes of plateaus. No matter what kind of scenery you like, Sichuan will never let you down!

Notes

1. 四川的交通承担着联系周边地区的重要责任。

"承担 (to undertake)" is a verb, which is commonly collocated with "~责任 (responsibility)、~义务 (duty)、~任务 (task/mission)、~工作 (work)". For example:

每个人都应该承担起保护环境的义务。

2. 到了夏天，很多住在四川东部的人会去西部，为的是躲开夏天的炎热；到了冬天，很多住在四川西部的人又会来四川东部，为的是躲开冬季的寒冷。

"……，为的是……" can be used to indicate purpose, as in "我把车停在外面，为的是走的时候方便". In this sentence, the purpose of "把车停在外面 (parking the car outside)" is "走的时候方便 (to be easier when leaving)".

Extensive Reading

Origin of the Name "Sichuan"

During the Northern Song Dynasty, a "lu" was roughly equivalent to a modern-day province. At that time, the goverment referred to the Sichuan Basin region as Chuanxia Lu. To strengthen administrative control, the Chuanxia Lu was later divided into Yizhou Lu, Zizhou Lu, Lizhou Lu and Kuizhou Lu, collectively known as the Chuanxia Si Lu, which eventually became simply known as "Sichuan".

Questions

1. Which part of China is Sichuan located in? What is the capital city of Sichuan province?

2. What are Sichuan's two typical landforms?

Experience

Where have you been to in Sichuan? Or do you want to visit Sichuan in the future? Which part(s) or region(s) is / are the most impressive to you?

Place(s) you have been to or want to visit in Sichuan	
Reason(s)	
Feature(s) of the place(s)	

（二）四川人是谁？

四川人起源于远古时期的巴族和蜀族，在漫长的历史中又不断与来自中国其他地区的移民相互融合。现在的四川人可以说是中国许多地方移民的后代。

让我们在历史上几次大规模的移民活动中追寻四川人的身份吧。秦国消灭蜀国后，曾经迁移了很多秦国的居民，也就是居住在现在陕西、甘肃一部分地区的民众进入四川；从唐末五代到南宋初年，大批北方人迁居蜀地；元末明初，南方移民大量进入四川；明末清初的大移民活动，也就是著名的"湖广填四川"，延续了一百多年；抗日战争时期，长江中下游居民不断进入四川；新中国成立后，大批北方干部进入四川；"三线建设"时期四川又迎来全国各地的人员……当然，更不必提人口流动更加频繁的当代，不同地区、不同国家的人来到四川，在此落地生根，安居乐业。

生活在移民的大家庭中，四川人形成了多样而复杂的性格特点。例如，四川人开放、包容的心态，全国闻名。"来的都是客！"这是四川人常说的一句话。四川是大家公认的中国最不排斥外来

第二眼看：
向世界讲述四川故事
Second Glance at Sichuan: Telling Sichuan Stories to the World

人口或外来文化的地区之一。宽容的心态自然带来"安逸"的生活态度！"安逸"这个词本来是四川方言，意思是"舒服"，但是现在已经因四川式舒服生活的影响力而进入普通话词汇了。

在历史上，四川是一个交通不便而又物产丰富的地方，所以在经济、文化等各方面形成了一个相对独立的区域。四川人则是出了名的"恋家"，不愿意离开四川，跟生活在中国沿海地区的人相比，有时显得比较缺乏冒险精神。但是，平时看起来安安逸逸、平平淡淡的四川人，到了历史的紧要关头，又能立刻显示出"敢为天下先"的勇气。在抗日战争中，近300万四川人加入了军队，川军的热血洒在了前线，留下了"无川不成军"的美名。同时，留在四川的人民则为国家承担了占总数三分之一的财政支出，为全国人民提供了占征收总量38.5%的稻谷……对四川人来说，追求安逸与勇敢善战其实并不矛盾，爱家所以爱国，爱生活所以爱人民，而正是因为热爱，才愿意牺牲所有换来和平。

四川还是一个多民族地区，有56个民族的人们共同生活在这里。其中，人数最多的几大民族是汉族、藏族、羌族和彝族。汉族是中国人口最多的民族，也是四川人口中占比最大的民族。但你可能还不知道，四川还是中国第二大藏族聚居区、唯一的羌族聚居区和第一大彝族聚居区。除此之外，在四川，还生活着苗族、壮族等少数民族。各民族人民相互交往，和睦相处，使四川的文化丰富多彩。

如果你来四川，千万不要错过去川西旅游的机会。川西，也就是四川西部，自古以来就是内地和西藏交往的通道，被称为"汉藏走廊"。在这里，生活着以藏族为主的六大民族。进入川西，蓝天白云下、草原河流间，五彩经幡在阳光和微风中特别引人注目。之所以叫"经幡",是因为这些小旗子上都写着佛经。在信仰藏传佛教的人们看来,经幡在风中飘动一下,就是诵读经文一次。微风中,经幡飘动,不停地向神传达人的愿望,求神保护。这里开阔的风景、独特的文化,都很值得旅行的人静下心来仔细品味。

阳光下的经幡

> **语言点例释**
>
> 1. 跟生活在中国沿海地区的人相比,四川人有时显得比较缺乏冒险精神。
>   "跟……相比"表示比较,例如"跟上次考试相比,这次没有那么难"。
> 2. 如果你来四川,千万不要错过去川西旅游的机会。
>   "错过"的意思是"失去(时机、对象)",例如"因为睡过头,我错过了公司的班车"。

第二眼看：
向世界讲述四川故事
Second Glance at Sichuan: Telling Sichuan Stories to the World

延伸阅读

文中各个历史时期的起止时间

秦国：前221—前206
唐朝：618—907
五代十国：907—960
南宋：1127—1279
元朝：1206—1368
明朝：1368—1644
清朝：1616—1911
抗日战争：1931—1945
"三线建设"时期：1964—1980

读后思考

1. 你能总结一下四川人的性格吗？这种性格的形成有哪些原因？

2. 居住在四川的少数民族中，哪几个民族的人数较多？

亲身体验

你有四川朋友吗？你会用哪些关键词来形容四川朋友的特点？为什么？

朋友的名字	最突出的个性	怎么认识的	交往中印象最深刻的事情

(2) Who Are the Sichuan People?

Sichuan people originated from the ancient Ba and Shu tribes and have continued to integrate with the migrants from other parts of China throughout the history. Today's Sichuan people are descendants of migrants across the country.

Several large-scale migrations in history have contributed to

the expansion of population in Sichuan. After the destruction of Shu State by Qin State, many residents of Qin State, living in parts of the present Shaanxi and Gansu provinces, entered Sichuan. Then, from the late Tang Dynasty and the Five dynasties to the early Southern Song Dynasty, a lot of northerners moved to this land. In late Yuan Dynasty and early Ming Dynasty, a large number of southern migrants poured into Sichuan. The great migration of the late Ming Dynasty and early Qing Dynasty lasted for more than a hundred years, known as "Hu-Guang filling in Sichuan" as the migrants mainly came from provinces such as Hunan, Hubei, Guangdong, and Guangxi. During the Chinese People's War of Resistance Against Japanese Aggression, residents of the middle and lower reaches of the Yangtze River stepped into Sichuan. After the founding of the People's Republic of China, plenty of northern cadres moved to Sichuan. During the "Third-Tier Construction" Period (the construction of infrastructure in the third-tier cities), Sichuan welcomed people all over the country... Nowadays, Sichuan has seen more and more people from different regions and countries settle down and start their lives here.

　　Living in a migration pot, Sichuan people have developed diverse and complex character traits. For example, people in Sichuan are famous for their open and inclusive attitude. "All who come are guests!" becomes a common saying in Sichuan. This province is widely recognized as one of the most inclusive areas of migrants and their cultures. Inclusiveness naturally leads to a relaxed life attitude among the locals. The expression "安逸(ānyì)" means "easy and comfortable". It was originally from

Second Glance at Sichuan: Telling Sichuan Stories to the World

the Sichuan dialect but has now been included in standard Chinese (Putonghua) vocabulary with the acceptance of Sichuan-style comfort.

Historically, Sichuan was a place with poor transportation but abundant products, so it was seen as a relatively independent space in terms of economy, culture and other aspects. People in Sichuan are known for being "attached to home" and unwilling to leave this land. Compared with those living in China's coastal areas, Sichuan people tend to be less adventurous. But Sichuan people, who usually seemed easeful and uneventful, showed their courage to "be the first in the world" at the critical moments in history. For instance, in the Chinese People's War of Resistance Against Japanese Aggression, nearly 3 million people in Sichuan joined the army. The Sichuan army fought against enemies on every inch of the war field, leaving the reputation of "no army without Sichuan people". At the same time, the people who stayed in Sichuan bore one-third of China's fiscal spending and provided 38.5% of the total rice expropriated... For Sichuan people, there is no contradiction between the pursuit of comfort and valiancy. They love their country because they love their families, and they love the people because they love their lives. And it is because of love that they are willing to sacrifice all for peace.

Sichuan is also a multi-ethnic region, with 56 ethnic groups living harmoniously together. Among them, Han ethnic group is the one with the largest population, and then are the ethnic group Zang, Qiang and Yi. Han is the most populous ethnic group not only in Sichuan but also in China. However, people may not know that Sichuan is also the second

largest habitation for Tibetans in China, the largest habitation for Yi people, and the only concentrated residential area for Qiang people. In addition, Miao, Zhuang and many other ethnic groups also live in Sichuan. People from different ethnic groups interact with each other and live in harmony, which makes Sichuan culture colorful and rich.

One should never miss the western Sichuan if they ever travel to Sichuan province. It is located in the western part of Sichuan, often referred to as "Han-Zang Corridor" which has connected the Tibetan region and southwestern China ever since the ancient times. Tibetans along with other five ethnic groups live in here. Under the blue sky and white clouds, along the rivers on the grasslands, the colorful prayer flags are really eye-catching in the sunshine and breeze. The "prayer flags" got their name for the sutras written on them. People who believe in Tibetan Buddhism think that the fluttering prayer flags are reciting sutras, conveying their wishes to gods for blessing. As for travelers, both the open views and unique culture are worthy of savoring.

Notes

1. 跟生活在中国沿海地区的人相比，四川人有时显得比较缺乏冒险精神。

"跟……相比" indicates comparison. For example: 跟上次考试相比，这次没有那么难。

2. 如果你来四川，千万不要错过去川西旅游的机会。

"错过" means "to miss (an opportunity, an object, etc.)". For example: 因为睡过头，我错过了公司的班车。

第二眼看四川：向世界讲述四川故事
Second Glance at Sichuan: Telling Sichuan Stories to the World

Extensive Reading

Historical Periods and Dates

Qin State: 221 BC – 206 BC

Tang Dynasty: 618 – 907

Five Dynasties and Ten Kingdoms: 907 – 960

Southern Song Dynasty: 1127 – 1279

Yuan Dynasty: 1206 – 1368

Ming Dynasty: 1368 – 1644

Qing Dynasty: 1616 – 1911

Chinese People's War of Resistance Against Japanese Aggression: 1931 – 1945

"Third-Tier Construction" Period: 1964 – 1980

Questions

1. Can you sum up the character traits of Sichuan people? Why do they develop such characters?

2. Please name the ethnic minorities with the largest population in Sichuan.

Experience

Please make a survey of your friend or someone from Sichuan to fill in the form.

Name of your friend	His/Her key personality	How did you know him/her?	The most impressive thing done by him/her

（三）四川怎么样？

如果要用关键词来形容四川，人们常常会选择"古老""发展"和"多元"三个词语。"古老"是说历史，"发展"是指现在，而"多元"则是说四川的文化。

四川这个地方，早在25 000年前就出现了人类文明。我们现在能够看到的宝墩文化、三星堆遗址、金沙遗址都是高度发达的古蜀文明的代表。古蜀文明与华夏文明、良渚文明并称为中国上古三大文明。在漫长的历史发展过程中，四川文化成为整个中华文化重要的部分。悠久的水利文化、著名的三国文化、丰富的宗教文化……悠久的历史一直是四川的一大魅力。在历史中形成的文化产品，例如蜀锦、川茶、竹编也都成为四川的"名片"。

四川不仅有辉煌的过去，更有快速发展的现在。从经济发展上看，2024年，四川省地区生产总值在全国居第五，在西部10个省中位列第一[1]。最新的统计数据显示，2024年，四川省地区生产总值为64 697亿元，比上年增长5.7%[2]。

最值得一提的是四川对外经济交往的发展。因为地处西南内陆，与东南沿海地区相比，四川省的对外经济交往开始得比较晚。但是近年来，在信息化发展的大背景下，四川的对外经济交往发展非常迅速。成都海关发布数据显示，2024年四川实现外贸进

1　千河奔腾风帆竞——四川坚定不移推动经济高质量发展观察. 四川省人民政府网 https://www.sc.gov.cn/10462/10464/10797/2025/4/27/949b2560d7c5469e9450cc38dc8e1b8f.shtml.

2　2024年四川二十一市（州）GDP出炉各市（州）如何以一域之力拼出发展合力. 四川省人民政府网.https://www.sc.gov.cn/10462/10464/10797/2025/2/1/b677ea0b450e4424bd6de4a7f274d0dc.shtml.

第二眼看四川：
向世界讲述四川故事
Second Glance at Sichuan: Telling Sichuan Stories to the World

出口10 457.2亿元，同比增长9.4%，高出全国4.4个百分点。[1]

最让四川人感到自豪的还是本地多元的文化。四川的文化一直有一种包容的气质。从古至今，四川曾经历了好几次大规模的战争和灾难，导致本地人口急剧下降。因此，四川历史上曾出现过几次较大的移民潮：从秦朝开始的李冰父子入川，到清初的"湖广填四川"，外来人口不断进入四川，和本地百姓融合，最终形成了四川的民族大融合。现在很多四川人去查自己的家谱，就会发现自己的祖辈都是从湖南、湖北、广东、广西等地方过来的。例如现在成都的洛带古镇就体现了典型的闽南文化，那里的很多居民依旧说客家话。在这样的背景下，加上四川人宽厚的性格，"排外"这种不喜欢外地人的做法，在四川是绝对不存在的。成都的导游常常会跟外地来的游客说，四川人很友好，大家出门玩，"路就在鼻子下面"啊！"路就在鼻子下面"的意思就是，如果你想问路，路边随便一个人都会很友好、很热情地告诉你的。

语言点例释

1. 最让四川人感到自豪的还是本地多元的文化。

　　这句话的大意是"多元文化让四川人感到自豪"。其中，"主语+让+人称代词+动词短语"的结构值得注意。这个结构中"让"的位置还可以使用"令、使、叫"等词语，例如"老师叫她早点儿回去"。

2. 从古至今，四川曾经历了好几次大规模的战争和灾难，导致本地人口急剧下降。

　　这句话的大意是"战争和灾难导致四川人口下降"。其中，"导致"是一个动词，意思是"引起"。需要注意的是，"导致"后面的情况一般是负面的，例如"一些小矛盾导致了他们的关系破裂"。

1　中华人民共和国成都海关.政府信息公开 chengdu customs.gov.cn/chengdu-cystoms/219425/fszdgknrl/bgti43/index.html。

延伸阅读

客家人

客家人是汉族的一支。一部分专家认为客家人本来是中原地区（大约相当于现在的河南省）的汉族人。他们在历史上经历了五次大规模的迁移，在南方多地逐渐形成汉民族的一个支系——客家。与其他移民不同的是，由于客家的先祖往往在交通不便的深山中居住，他们原有的语言、风俗和文化没有受到其他文化的深刻影响，从而保留下来，并以自己独特的方式慢慢演变。

读后思考

1. 四川从什么时候开始出现了人类文明？
2. 对于四川的多元文化，你有没有具体的例子来说明？

亲身体验

去洛带古镇走一走，你一定能感受到客家文化的个性。请试试先体验再补充下表：

向世界讲述四川故事

Second Glance at Sichuan: Telling Sichuan Stories to the World

体验客家文化	你知道吗？
特色建筑	下图中建筑的名字是 _____。 这样的建筑有什么功能？ _____。
特色饮食	下图中这道菜叫作 _____。 这道菜有什么来历？ _____。
特色方言	试着听听当地人聊天，能听懂吗？和普通话或成都话一样吗？

(3) How Is Sichuan?

If one is asked to describe Sichuan in a few keywords, the following three may immediately come to mind: ancient, growing, and diverse. "Ancient" refers to the long history, "growing" indicates the present development, and "diverse" is the social and cultural character of Sichuan.

As early as 25,000 years ago, human civilization emerged in Sichuan. Baodun Cultural Relics, Sanxingdui Ruin Site and Jinsha Relics, which we have discovered today, are all extraordinary representations of the highly developed ancient Sichuan Civilization, also called Ancient Shu Civilization. The civilizations of ancient Shu,

Huaxia (ancient Chinese) and Liangzhu are known as the three great civilizations in Ancient China. Throughout the long history, Sichuan culture has become a significant component of Chinese culture. Sichuan's charm lies in its splendid history featuring the time-honored water conservancy culture, the famous Three Kingdoms Culture, diverse religions... The cultural products created during the past times, such as Shu Jin, Sichuan tea and bamboo weaving, have all become Sichuan's "name tags".

Sichuan boasts not only a glorious past, but also a rapid development at present. From the perspective of economic growth, the GDP of Sichuan ranked the fifth in China and the first among the 10 western provinces in 2024. In the same year, according to the latest statistics, Sichuan's GDP was 64, 697 trillion *yuan*, an increase of 5.7% over the previous year.

One of the most impressive aspects of Sichuan's economy is its economic cooperation with foreign countries. Because of being located at a geographical backwater in southwest China, the foreign economic cooperation in Sichuan, compared with the southeast coastal areas, got a relatively late start. But in recent years, with the development of information technology, Sichuan's economic cooperation with the world has seen dramatic growth. The data released by Chengdu Customs shows that in 2024, Sichuan achievde a total foreign trade import and export value of 1.04572 trillion *yuan*, a year-on-year increase of 9.4%, 4.4 percentage points higher than the national average.

However, what makes the locals most proud of is their diverse

culture. Sichuan culture has always been an inclusive one. Since ancient times, Sichuan has undergone several large-scale wars and disasters, resulting in sharp declines in the local population. Luckily, the province has witnessed several massive migration waves in the history: from Libing and his son with migrant workers settling down here in the Qin Dynasty, to the migration of "Hu-Guang filling in Sichuan", the migrants kept pouring into Sichuan, integrated with the locals, and finally, shaped Sichuan into such a great place of ethnic fusion. Hence, for most Sichuan people, if they look up in their genealogical books, they may find that their ancestors were all from Hu-Guang areas (including provinces such as Hunan, Hubei, Guangdong, and Guangxi). For example, the Luodai Ancient Town in Chengdu is a typical representative of Minnan (Southern areas of Fujian province) culture, where people still speak Hakka. With such colorful cultures, Sichuan people, coupled with their generosity, will be absolutely inclusive to the non-natives. Many tour guides in Chengdu often say to visitors, "If you ask for directions, anyone on the street would like to tell you very warmly. And this is literally called 'the way is under your nose'."

Notes

1. 最让四川人感到自豪的还是本地多元的文化。

　　This sentence basically means "多元文化让四川人感到自豪", in which the structure of "subject + 让 + personal pronoun + verb phrase" should be kept in mind. Here "让" can be substituted for some other causative verbs like "令、使、叫". For example:

　　老师叫她早点儿回去。

2. 从古至今，四川曾经历了好几次大规模的战争和灾难，导致本地人口急剧下降。

　　This sentence basically means "战争和灾难导致四川人口下降". Here, "导致" is a verb which means "to cause". It is important to note that the situation after "导致" is generally negative. For example:

　　一些小矛盾导致了他们关系的破裂。

Extensive Reading

Hakkas

　　The Hakkas are a branch of the Han people. Some experts believe that the Hakkas were originally Han people from central China (today's Henan province). They experienced five large-scale migrations throughout the history, and gradually formed a unique branch of the Han ethnic group in many southern areas—Hakka. Unlike other migrants, the ancestors of the Hakka people often lived in remote mountains with inconvenient transportation. Therefore, their original language, customs and culture were not significantly affected by other cultures, but remained intact and slowly evolved in their own unique way.

Questions

1. When did the human civilization emerge in Sichuan?

2. Do you have any specific example of the diverse cultures of Sichuan?

Experience

Take a walk in the Luodai Ancient Town and you will surely feel the uniqueness of Hakka culture. Please try to fill in the following form based on your experience:

Experience of Hakka Culture	Do you know these?
Distinctive Architecture	The name of the building in the picture below is _____. What function does such a building serve? _____.
Special Food	The dish below is called _____. What's the origin of this dish? _____.
Unique Dialect	Try to listen to and understand a locals' chatting. Is it the same as standard Chinese (Putonghua) or Chengdu dialect?

（四）四川话啥样？

既然有那么多个民族，那在四川你能听到的语言也是非常丰富的，有汉语、藏语、彝语等。这里，我们先聊聊汉语。如果你会普通话，那么你在四川会听到一种跟普通话类似但又不完全一样的汉语，那就是"四川话"。四川话是汉语的一种方言。我们

都知道,普通话是以中国的北方方言为基础的,而四川话就是一种北方方言,所以跟普通话的关系很近,只是在语音和词汇方面有一些小小的不同。如果你第一次听四川话,一时没有听懂,可以请对方再说一次,请对方慢慢地讲,这样你就能够明白大概的意思了。当然,现在四川和中国其他地方一样,大部分人都会说普通话。在学校、公安局、银行等单位,工作人员都必须说标准普通话,所以完全用不着担心"听不懂四川话怎么交流"这个问题。但是当你办完事情,悠闲地走入某条小街,遇到几位热情的爷爷或是阿姨,你可能会听到一种很"可爱"的普通话发音。这种发音被中国人称为"椒盐普通话"。"椒"是指花椒,"椒盐"是很有特色的四川菜的一种味道,所以中国其他地方的人就用这种味道形容四川人的有点怪怪的普通话发音,来开四川人的玩笑。之所以会有这种"椒盐普通话",可能也是因为四川话和普通话太像了,所以四川人有时候会弄不清楚,这个音到底是四川话的还是普通话的。

很多外国朋友刚听到四川话的时候,会觉得说话的人在吵架。这是因为四川话说起来语调上升和下降的幅度比较大,而且节奏也比较急,听起来有点生气的感觉。但听上一段时间,我保证你也能发现四川话的魅力。四川话中有很多叠音词,比如"绳绳"(绳子)、"盖盖"(盖子),还常常使用语气词,比如"啦""哈"。这些有特色的语言现象,让四川人在讲话的时候很有感染力。

现在不仅是四川人深爱自己的方言,中国其他地方的人们也学会了欣赏四川话的魅力。一个有力的证明是很多电视剧和电影里面都会设计一个说四川话或者"椒盐普通话"的人物,专门负责幽默卖萌。有人说,四川话和东北话、上海话、广东话是中

第二眼看 ：
向世界讲述四川故事
Second Glance at Sichuan: Telling Sichuan Stories to the World

国影视剧中应用最广的方言。网友们还因此总结出四川话的幽默"三大法宝"：第一，四川话很喜欢使用叠词给东西取名字，例如"鱼"就叫"鱼摆摆"，请"脑补"一下鱼游起来摆摆尾巴的样子；第二，四川话喜欢拖长音加语气词，例如"你好——乖哦"，有的外地朋友觉得这样的发音简直就像熊猫一样可爱；第三，四川话里面的形容词非常多，例如要说什么东西很软，四川人不会只说"软"，而是会说"耙溜溜的"，"耙"就是"软"，"溜溜"则兼顾了很滑的感觉。

语言点例释

1. 完全用不着担心"听不懂四川话怎么交流"这个问题。
   "用不着"是一个固定短语，意思是"不用，不需要"，例如"你有话可以直接说，用不着害怕"。
2. 中国其他地方的人们也学会了欣赏四川话的魅力。
   "欣赏"是一个动词，在这句话中的意思是"认为好，喜欢"，例如"他很欣赏这座建筑的中式风格"。除了这个意思，"欣赏"还有"享受美好的事物"的意思，例如"欣赏音乐，欣赏风景"。

延伸阅读

脑补

"脑补"是一个汉语网络流行语。文章中的意思是指在阅读时，自己对一些情节进行补充和想象。

读后思考

1. 四川有哪些少数民族？
2. 四川话有什么特点？你知道哪些四川话的词语？从哪里知道的？

亲身体验

先猜一猜这些词用四川话怎么说，然后问问来自四川的老师

或者朋友，将会得到惊喜的答案哦！

普通话	可以	太好了	知道	说话	膝盖	蜻蜓
四川话						

交流讨论

分享一下你最常听到的一个四川话词语或者句子。

四川话词语或者句子	什么意思	什么时候在哪里听到的

(4) What Is Sichuan Dialect?

Since there are so many ethnic groups in Sichuan, the languages or dialects there are indeed diverse, including Han Chinese language, Tibetan, Yi language, etc. First, let's talk about Han Chinese language. In Sichuan, you may hear a type of Chinese that is similar to Putonghua but not exactly the same. This is known as "Sichuan dialect". It is one dialect of Chinese language. As is known to all, Putonghua is based on the Chinese northern dialects, and Sichuan dialect is a branch of northern dialects. Therefore, it sounds very similar to Putonghua, but with some subtle differences in phonetics and vocabulary. If one can't get it when first hearing Sichuan dialect, it's okay to ask locals to repeat it for a better understanding. Nowadays, most people in Sichuan, like the rest of China, can certainly speak Putonghua. Moreover, the staff or faculty in schools, police stations, banks and other institutions are required to speak Putonghua, so there is no need to worry about the language barrier in Sichuan. However, when coming across some

friendly seniors, one may hear a quite cute version of Putonghua, which is called "椒盐普通话 (jiāoyán pǔtōnghuà)". "椒 (jiāo)" and "盐 (yán)" refer to Sichuan pepper and salt respectively, and "椒盐 (jiaoyán)" is a very distinctive flavor of Sichuan cuisine. As time went on, people in other parts of China have started to use this flavor to describe such a lovely pronunciation of Sichuan people, just for fun. The reason why "椒盐普通话" exists is perhaps that Sichuan dialect and Putonghua are so alike that Sichuan people themselves sometimes can't figure out whether the sound is from the dialect or Putonghua.

Many foreigners may think the locals are quarreling when they first hear the Sichuan dialect. This is because the tones of the dialect rise and drop sharply, and its rhythm is usually fast, making the speaker sound slightly crossed. But after a while, they will absolutely find beauty in Sichuan dialect. It has many reiteratives like "绳绳 (shéngsheng)" and "盖盖 (gàigai)", which are "绳子 (shéngzi)" and "盖子 (gàizi)" respectively in Putonghua; furthermore, modal particles are used frequently such as "哈 (ha)" or "啦 (la)". Such distinctive linguistic phenomena make Sichuan people infectious when speaking Sichuan dialect.

Now it's not just Sichuan people who love their own dialect, but people in other parts across the nation have also known how to appreciate the charms of Sichuan dialect. A good example of this is that many TV series and movies often create a unique character with Sichuan dialect or "椒盐普通话" to be specifically responsible for humor or cuteness. It is said that Sichuan dialect, along with the dialect

of northeast China, Shanghainese and Cantonese, are the most widely used dialects in Chinese films and TV series. Hence, the netizens have summed up three magic keys of the humor of Sichuan dialect. Firstly, it often uses reiteratives to name items. For example, "鱼 (yú)" is called "鱼摆摆 (yú bǎibai)". Secondly, it usually adds modal particles in a long drawl, such as "你好——乖哦！(you are sooooo cute!)". Some foreign friends think this kind of cute pronunciation is just as lovely as a panda. And thirdly, there are many adjectives in Sichuan dialect. For instance, Sichuan people tend to use the phrase "耙溜溜的 (pá liū liū de)" instead of "软 (ruǎn)" in Putonghua to describe that something is very soft. In this case, "耙" means "soft" and "溜溜" indicates "smoothness".

Notes

1. 完全用不着担心"听不懂四川话怎么交流"这个问题。

"用不着" is a fixed phrase meaning "don't need to". For example:

你有话可以直接说，用不着害怕。

2. 中国其他地方的人们也学会了欣赏四川话的魅力。

"欣赏" is a verb that in this sentence means "to think well of, or to like". For example:

他很欣赏这座建筑的中式风格。

Besides this, "欣赏" also means "to enjoy something beautiful". For example:

欣赏音乐 / 欣赏风景

Extensive Reading

Headcanon

Headcanon, "脑补 (nǎo bǔ)" in standard Chinese, is a Chinese internet buzzword. In this article it refers to someone's personal interpretation, imagination or belief of the details or plots in an article while reading.

· 27 ·

第二眼看 ：

向世界讲述四川故事

Second Glance at Sichuan: Telling Sichuan Stories to the World

 Questions

1. What ethnic minorities are there in Sichuan?

2. What are the features of Sichuan dialect? Do you know any word or expression of Sichuan dialect? And how did you know it?

Experience

First guess how people say the following words in Sichuan dialect, and then ask your teachers or friends for the right answers.

Mandarin	OK	awesome	know	speak	knee	dragonfly
Sichuan Dialect						

Discussion

Please share one word or sentence in Sichuan dialect that you frequently hear.

Word/Sentence	What does it mean?	When and where do you usually hear it?

二、自然篇

小熊猫是小的大熊猫吗？牛奶海跟牛奶有什么关系？光雾山为什么有那么多的雾？……本篇为你讲述四个不可思议的自然故事。

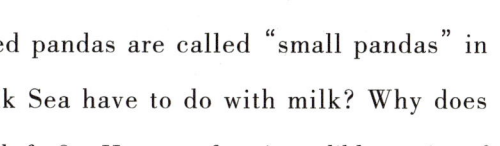

2. Nature

Do you know that red pandas are called "small pandas" in Chinese? What does Milk Sea have to do with milk? Why does Guangwushan have so much fog?... Here are four incredible stories of nature in this chapter.

第二眼看四川：向世界讲述四川故事
Second Glance at Sichuan: Telling Sichuan Stories to the World

（一）童话世界——九寨沟自然保护区

汉语中有句话叫作"九寨归来不看水"，意思是如果你去九寨沟旅游过，那其他的江河和湖泊都不用再去了，因为没有比这里的水更美的了。当然，这句话比较夸张，但是也显示了人们对九寨沟的赞美。九寨沟的"寨"不是一个常见的汉字，简单地说就是指村子。九寨沟这个名字就来自保护区里面的九个藏族寨子。这些藏族人民世世代代居住在这里，过着自给自足的生活。他们把雪山看成男神和女神，认为湖泊就是女神用来洗脸的盆子，而漫山遍野的树木则是女神的长发。正是由于这种崇敬自然的态度，九寨沟成为各种动物和植物的美好家园。

九寨沟的美景

九寨沟位于四川省西北部，是阿坝藏族羌族自治州的一部分。这里距离成都市400多千米，是嘉陵江上游的一条大支沟。沟里地势高低差别很大，北面的沟口海拔仅2000米，中部均在4000米以上，南面则有4500米以上。整条沟长30多千米，分布着成群的湖泊和瀑布，因各种地质原因而表现出多种色彩，就好像是童话的世界一样！九寨沟是中国第一个以保护自然风景为主要目

的的自然保护区。

九寨沟的发现很有传奇色彩。1966年,一群负责砍树的工人来到这里。他们走进森林深处,惊叹于眼前的童话世界。这些工人将拍摄的美景照片带出九寨沟后,引起了人们的广泛注意。四川省政府随即组织专家对九寨沟进行考察,认为"九寨沟不仅有丰富、珍贵的动植物资源,也是世界上少有的优美景区",开始对这里进行保护。1978年,中央政府批准建立了九寨沟国家级自然保护区。1992年,这一保护区被列入"世界自然遗产名录"。

九寨沟以湖泊和瀑布闻名世界,其中最美丽的要算"五彩池"这个最小、颜色却最丰富的湖。五彩池海拔2995米,深6.6米,藏在深谷中。五彩池里的水清澈见底,我们完全可以透过池水看到池底石头上的花纹。最为神奇的是,冬天气温极低,周围一片冰天雪地,这里的池水依然清波荡漾,而且无论是雨季还是旱季,池水都不会增加或者减少。这是因为五彩池的水源来自地下,因而一年四季都能保持一样的温度和水量。站在五彩池边放眼望去,同一湖泊里,有的地方蔚蓝,有的地方浅绿,有的水带着黄色,有的则是可爱的粉蓝……真是变化无穷!这又是为什么呢?如果细心观看,我们可以看到五彩池的水里生长着水绵、轮藻、小蕨等水生植物,芦苇、节节草、水灯芯等草本植物。这些植物的绿色深浅不同,倒映在湖水中就呈现出不同的颜色。加上池底石头的花纹色彩,本来蓝色的湖面变得五彩斑斓。因此,精致的五彩池也被大家称为"九寨之眼"。

童话世界中不仅有美景,也有奇妙的动物。这里生活着一种很像猫的小动物,全身红褐色,圆圆的脸上有白色的斑纹,还拖着一条又粗又长的尾巴。它们猫脸熊身,似猫非猫,似熊非熊,

第二眼看：
向世界讲述四川故事
Second Glance at Sichuan: Telling Sichuan Stories to the World

被叫作"小熊猫"。小熊猫的性格机警，但是很温顺。它们活动灵活，特别善于爬树，爱吃竹叶、果实、小鸟等。小熊猫一半像猫一半像熊，而九寨沟里另一种特别的动物——羚牛则是"六不像"。什么叫"六不像"？羚牛样子像牛，其实是一种羊，是世界上公认的珍贵动物之一，在中国被列为国家一级保护动物。它们体形粗壮，大约有2.1米长，300公斤重，好像一头小水牛，但是头很小，尾巴短。它们叫起来像羊，还偏偏长了一张长脸，跟马一模一样。这么奇怪的样子把大家都搞糊涂了，干脆就叫它们"六不像"。羚牛的角最特别，从头部长出后突然翻转向外侧伸出，然后折向后方，看起来很扭曲，所以科学家称它们为"扭角羚"。

那么这个童话世界是怎么形成的呢？科学家解释说，九寨沟的许多地貌景观，如湖泊、瀑布等，其实都是这个地区不断发生的地震带来的。危险的灾害造就了令人惊叹的美丽，大自然就是这么奇妙！2017年九寨沟发生了7.0级地震，很多景观遭到了破坏，一些植被被摧毁。但是研究人员发现，一些新的景观正在开始形成。例如"火花海"这个湖泊被破坏了，但是湖泊中的水大量排放，使下游的"双龙海"湖泊面积扩大，形成了气势磅礴的"双龙海"瀑布。让人庆幸的是，经过自然的修复和人们精心的保护，现在九寨沟核心景区的植被生态景观已恢复到了地震以前的水平。

谢天谢地，童话世界还在！

自然篇
Nature

小熊猫

羚牛

🌺 语言点例释 🌺

1. 他们走进森林深处，惊叹于眼前的童话世界。

　　这句话的大意是"人们对森林深处的童话世界感到惊叹"。介词"于"相当于"对"，带有书面色彩。

2. 现在九寨沟核心景区的植被生态景观已恢复到了地震以前的水平。

　　这句话的大意是"现在九寨沟的生态景观已经恢复"。其中，"恢复"是一个动词，意思是"变回原来的样子"，例如"他的健康已经完全恢复"。

第二眼看四川：向世界讲述四川故事
Second Glance at Sichuan: Telling Sichuan Stories to the World

读后思考

1. 人们为什么说"九寨归来不看水"？
2. 人们为什么把羚牛叫作"六不像"？

交流讨论

让人恐惧的自然灾难造出了令人惊叹的美景，你如何理解大自然的力量以及人与自然的关系？

亲身体验

在九寨沟旅游时，请拍下你觉得最让人惊叹的美丽风景，并且查阅资料说一说这样的风景是怎样形成的。

(1) Jiuzhaigou National Park: A Fairyland

There is a Chinese saying "九寨归来不看水 (Jiǔzhài guīlái bú kàn shuǐ)", which literally means that one doesn't even wish to visit any other places after returning from Jiuzhaigou National Park, because its water scenery tops those elsewhere. This saying is, of course, a bit exaggerative, but it also shows people's praise of Jiuzhaigou. The character "寨 (zhài)" is not a common one, which simply means village. Actually, the name "Jiuzhaigou" came from the nine Tibetan stockaded villages in the reserve. Those Tibetans have lived there for generations, leading a self-sufficient life. They regard the snow mountains as gods and goddesses, the lakes as the washbasins of the goddesses, and the trees all over the mountains as their long hair. It is because of such respect for nature that Jiuzhaigou has become a wonderful home for all kinds of animals and plants.

自然篇
Nature

Jiuzhaigou, located in Aba Tibetan and Qiang Autonomous Prefecture in the northwest of Sichuan province, more than 400 kilometers away from Chengdu, is a large branch of the upper reaches of Jialing River. With the various and complex terrain, the altitude of Jiuzhaigou descends from its high south of over 4,500 meters to the low north of only 2,000 meters, with middle areas above 4,000 meters. The whole valley is over 30 kilometers long, with numerous lakes and waterfalls in the middle, demonstrates bright colors for various geographical reasons, just like a fairyland! Jiuzhaigou is the first nature reserve in China that aims to protect natural scenery.

The discovery of Jiuzhaigou is legendary. In 1966, a group of loggers came here and marveled at this fairyland as going deeper into the forest. So they showed the world photos of beautiful scenery in Jiuzhaigou, having attracted widespread attention. Seeing that, the people's government of Sichuan province immediately organized experts to investigate this area, believing that "Jiuzhaigou is not only with abundant and precious resources of animals and plants, but also a rare scenic spot in the world". Therefore, a significant protection project started. In 1978, the central government approved the establishment of Jiuzhaigou National Nature Reserve, which was later added to the UNESCO World Natural Heritage List in 1992.

Jiuzhaigou is famous for its lakes and waterfalls, among which the most beautiful is the Five-Color Pond, the smallest but most colorful lake. This lake is at an altitude of 2,995 meters with a depth of 6.6

meters, hidden in a deep valley, in which the water is so clear that the patterns on the stones at the bottom are visible. And it is most amazing that even in freezing and snowy winter, the lake still ripples, with a constant water level regardless of weather conditions. This is because the water in the lake comes from underground, which remains a constant temperature and water volume all year round. Standing by the lake and looking down, one will see various colors like blue, light green, yellow and lovely powder-blue in the same lake, full of endless changes! Why is that? It can be observed that the lake is full of spirogyra, rotunda, small ferns and other aquatic plants, as well as reeds, grass, water wick and other herbs. Different green shades of these plants are reflected in gorgeous colors in the lake; along with the patterns and colors of stones at the bottom, the originally blue lake turns colorful. Therefore, the exquisite Five-Color Pond is also known as the "Eye of Jiuzhai".

The fairyland not only presents beautiful sceneries, but also lives wonderful animals. Here lives a small, cat-like animal, entirely reddish-brown, with white markings on its round face and a long, bushy tail. The red panda has a cat-like face and a bear-like body, but much smaller than a giant panda, so it is called "小熊猫 (xiǎo xióngmāo)" in Chinese, literally meaning "small panda". Red pandas are alert but docile. They climb trees with agility, and subsist mainly on bamboo, fruits, and little birds. And in Jiuzhaigou there is another special animal—the takin. Recent DNA studies have placed the takin closer to sheep. It is widely identified as a rare species and a national first-class protected animal in China. It is robust, about 2.1

meters long and weighing about 300 kilograms, looking like a small buffalo, but with a smaller head and a shorter tail. Its voice, however, sounds like sheep bleating, while its face is as long as a horse. Such strange appearance easily confuse people, so they are nicknamed "六不像 (liù bú xiàng)" in Chinese, which literally means "unlike the other six animals". They have heavy horns that turn outward from the centre of the forehead and then curve up and backward, so Chinese scientists call them "twisted-horn antelope".

So how did this fairyland come into being? According to scientists, many landforms in Jiuzhaigou, such as lakes and waterfalls, are actually resulted by constant earthquakes in this area. Nature is so wonderful that even dangerous disasters have left such an amazing beauty! In 2017, a 7.0-magnitude earthquake struck Jiuzhaigou, having destroyed many landscapes and vegetation in some areas. However, at the same time researchers also found that some new landscapes were created. For instance, the Sparkling Lake was damaged, but a massive water discharge of the lake made the Shuanglong Lake downstream expand in size and thus form the magnificent Shuanglong Waterfall. Very fortunately, after the natural restoration and people's careful preservation, the vegetation ecological landscapes of Jiuzhaigou's core areas has been gradually returned to the pre-earthquake level.

Thank goodness the fairyland is still there!

第二眼看四川：
向世界讲述四川故事
Second Glance at Sichuan: Telling Sichuan Stories to the World

🞻 Notes 🞻

1. 他们走进森林深处，惊叹于眼前的童话世界。

The general meaning of this sentence is: "People are amazed at the fairytale world deep in the forest."

The preposition "于" is equivalent to "at" or "toward" in this context, and it carries a formal, literary tone.

2. 现在九寨沟核心景区的植被生态景观已恢复到了地震以前的水平。

This sentence basically means "现在九寨沟的生态景观已经恢复". Here, "恢复" is a verb which means "to recover". For example:

他的健康已经完全恢复。

🞻 Questions 🞻

1. Why do people say "九寨归来不看水？
2. Why do people call takins "六不像" in Chinese?

🞻 Discussion 🞻

How do you understand the power of nature and the relationship between man and nature?

🞻 Experience 🞻

When traveling in Jiuzhaigou, please take photos of the amazing sceneries that impress you most and try to explain how they were formed.

（二）"滚滚"的家——卧龙自然保护区

"滚滚"是中国网民对大熊猫的爱称，是不是很形象？这个胖乎乎的大个子可不就是整天滚来滚去的吗？大熊猫可以说是四川最受欢迎的一张"名片"了。四川人民对它们可不仅是喜爱，更为保护它们和它们的"家"做出了巨大的努力和贡献。其中，

自然篇
Nature

位于四川汶川县的卧龙自然保护区就是一个特别好的例子。

卧龙自然保护区1963年成立，开启了四川的大熊猫保护事业。因为效果特别好，1978年这里被中央政府定为首个国家级大熊猫自然保护区。最值得一提的是，1980年卧龙保护区加入了联合国教科文组织"人与生物圈"保护区网，开始探索新型管理方法，以实现"人与自然和谐共生"。简单来说，就是在严格保护保护区的动物的同时，也解决在保护区内居住的几千人的生活问题，让动物和人和谐地共同生活。

你见过大熊猫滑雪吗？在冬天的卧龙，有时候能看到大熊猫在雪地缓坡"哧溜"一下滑下去。原来呀，滚滚也怕冷，这是运动取暖呢！大熊猫一般在晚上11点左右休息，每隔3个小时就起来运动。这时它们满身都是冰雪，走起路来叮叮当当的，真是可爱得不得了！

大熊猫

除了保护大熊猫，卧龙保护区还有保护金丝猴等其他动物的任务。卧龙地区海拔落差极大，横跨6个气候垂直带，拥有多样的生物种类，是世界上宝贵的生物基因库。同时，由于保护区位于成都平原的西北边缘，地理位置特殊，这里的森林可以很好地阻挡西北风，保护四川不受冰冷北风的伤害。因此，这个保护区真的是保护了从动物到人再到整个四川的生态安全。

2018年，卧龙保护区内的红外相机先后拍到了雪豹和金钱豹，还记录下三只黑熊幼崽一起玩耍的有趣画面。对此，科学家们认为，金钱豹与雪豹两种大型猫科动物在同一地区生活，说明卧龙保护区已经有效地保存下当地完整、健康的生态系统，为这片区域内所有的野生动植物提供了自由生活的家园。

这一消息让四川人民既开心又骄傲，要知道这一结果可是来之不易！卧龙保护区的生态环境曾在2008年"5·12"汶川特大地震中受到严重破坏。为了使滚滚和其他动植物能有一个安全的生活环境，卧龙森林消防中队和保护区管理局全力以赴地工作，终于在两年后完成了对保护区和大熊猫研究中心的重建。

现在，保护区早已恢复了往日的宁静，迎接来自四面八方的游客。这里离成都市中心大约120千米，交通方便。保护区内年平均气温8.9摄氏度，人们春季可以赏雪观花，夏天避暑休闲，秋季观林尝果，冬季体验大雪满山的好风光。离保护区不远的耿达镇和卧龙镇还有各具特色的"农家乐"，供游客休息和住宿。

在保护区的"中华大熊猫苑"，大家不仅可以近距离观赏大熊猫，还可以成为志愿者为大熊猫服务。"大熊猫博物馆"更是详尽地展示了大熊猫家族的历史和近30年人类对大熊猫的保护与研究。如果喜欢户外运动，你还可以在原始森林中观察滚滚家

的自然环境,协助大熊猫保护工作者对大熊猫进行追踪,学习设置红外相机和收集数据,真是既有趣,又有意义!

语言点例释

1. 这时它们满身都是冰雪,走起路来叮叮当当的,真是可爱得不得了!

"不得了"表示程度很深,可以用在动词或者形容词后面作补语,与"非常地,极其地"意思相近,例如"他考试得了第一名,高兴得不得了!"。

2. "大熊猫博物馆"更是详尽地展示了大熊猫家族的历史和近30年人类对大熊猫的保护与研究。

"展示"是一个动词,在这句话中的意思是"清楚地摆出来",例如"这次活动展示了公司的最新产品"。除了这个意思,"展示"还有"明显地表现出来"的意思,例如"这个作品展示了人物的内心活动"。

拓展阅读

滚滚降级啦

2021年,滚滚成功"降级",从"濒危"变为"易危"动物。这可是个好消息!现在中国的生态环境越来越好,中国人也越来越重视环境与动物保护,因此大熊猫和其他很多野生动物一样,数量得到了很大的增长。有网友表示:"离人手一只圆滚滚的日子又近了一步。"这当然是玩笑话,"易危"并不代表就可以减少对滚滚的保护。事实上,滚滚已经成为很多动物的"保护伞",人们在保护滚滚的同时也保护了其他动物和当地的生态。

读后思考

1. 中国网民为什么把大熊猫叫作"滚滚"?

2. 在你的国家,大熊猫受欢迎吗?你觉得大家为什么如此喜欢大熊猫?

交流讨论

曾经有条新闻说,一位外国网友以为四川人家里都有一只大

熊猫,人们出门都遛"熊猫",现实当然不是这样的。你到中国之前对中国有哪些误解?之后又是如何消除这些误解的?请与你的同伴分享一下。

(2) Wolong Nature Reserve: Home of Giant Pandas

"滚滚 (gǔngun)", literally meaning "to roll", is the nickname given by Chinese netizens for giant pandas. Isn't it a very vividly descriptive name? And aren't those big chubby creatures just rolling around all day? The giant panda is arguably the most popular name tag of Sichuan. Sichuan people not only love them, but also make great efforts and contributions to protect them as well as their "home". The Wolong Nature Reserve in Wenchuan County sets a particularly good example.

Wolong Nature Reserve was established in 1963, embarking on giant panda conservation in Sichuan. It was so effective that in 1978 this place was designated by the central government as the first national nature reserve for giant pandas. Most notably, in 1980, Wolong Nature Reserve was added to Reserve Network of Man and Biosphere by UNESCO, and began to explore new management to achieve "harmony between humanity and nature". To put it simply, it means not only strict protection of animals in the reserve, but also a solution to living problems facing by the local residents.

Have you ever seen a giant panda skiing? On winter days in Wolong, giant pandas may sometimes roll down a snow slope to keep

warm. They usually sleep around 11 p.m. and may wake up to play every three hours. And then they will get covered with ice and snow, walking like a big snowball. Truly lovely!

Besides giant pandas, there are many other rare animals such as golden sub-nosed monkeys in this reserve. The Wolong region has a significant variation in altitude, stretching across six vertical climate zones, which results in a diverse range of biological species. It serves as a valuable genetic bank for biodiversity in the world. Additionally, due to a unique geographical position—on the northwest edge of the Chengdu Plain—the forests in this area effectively block the northwest wind, protecting Sichuan from the cold northern winds. Therefore, this nature reserve plays a crucial role in safeguarding the animals, humans, and the entire Sichuan region ecology.

In 2018, infrared cameras set up in Wolong Nature Reserve captured snow leopards and Chinese leopards, as well as three black bear cubs playing together. This discovery, said by scientists, can demonstrate the comprehensive and healthy ecosystem of Wolong Nature Reserve, providing a wonderful homeland for all wildlife.

Sichuan people were extremely happy and proud to hear this piece of exciting news that was indeed hard-won. Unfortunately, the ecological environment of Wolong Nature Reserve was severely damaged in 5/12 Wenchuan Earthquake in 2008. In order to provide a safe living environment for giant pandas and other wildlife, Wolong local authorities and forest firefighters worked so hard that they finally completed the reconstruction of the reserve and the Giant Panda

Research Center two years later.

Now, the reserve has restored tranquility and started to receive visitors throughout the world. It is about 120 kilometers away from Chengdu, with very convenient transportation. The annual average temperature in the reserve is 8.9℃, hence people can appreciate both snow and flowers in spring, enjoy the summer travel and recreation, taste fruits and enjoy forests in fall, and experience the beautiful snowy mountains in winter. In addition, the towns of Gengda and Wolong, not far from the reserve, host the distinctive "agritainment", which offer recreations and lodging for visitors.

In the Chinese Giant Panda Park of the reserve, you can not only see the pandas up close, but also serve as volunteers for them. And the Giant Panda Museum displays the history of the giant panda family and the conservation as well as research on them in the past 30 years in details. People who like outdoor activities, can explore the primary forests to observe the natural environment of giant pandas, assist the staff to track the pandas, or learn to set up infrared cameras and collect data, which can be really interesting and meaningful!

自然篇
Nature

🙞 Notes 🙜

1. 这时它们满身都是冰雪，走起路来叮叮当当的，真是可爱得不得了！

"不得了" can be used after a verb or adjective as a complement to emphasize degree, which means "awfully and extremely". For example:

他考试得了第一名，高兴得不得了！

2. "大熊猫博物馆"更是详尽地展示了大熊猫家族的历史和近30年人类对大熊猫的保护与研究。

"展示" is a verb, in this sentence meaning "to exhibit, to display, or to show". For example:

这次活动展示了公司的最新产品。

Besides, "展示" also means "to reveal". For example:

这个作品展示了人物的内心活动。

🙞 Extensive Reading 🙜

Giant Panda Got off Endangered List

Good news! In 2021, Chinese conservation officials have announced that the giant panda has been successfully downgraded from "endangered" to "vulnerable" on the global list of species at risk of extinction. As China's ecological environment is getting better and better and Chinese people are paying more and more attention to the environment and animal protection, the population of giant pandas, like many other wild animals, has increased significantly. "It's one step closer to the day that everyone can have a chubby giant panda," joked by a netizen. "Vulnerable" does not indicate to give less protection to pandas. In fact, the giant panda has become an "protective umbrella" for many other animals as well as the local ecology.

🙞 Questions 🙜

1. Why do Chinese netizens call the giant panda "滚滚"?

2. Are pandas popular in your home country? Why do people like pandas so much?

第二眼看四川：
向世界讲述四川故事
Second Glance at Sichuan: Telling Sichuan Stories to the World

Discussion

There was once a piece of interesting news saying that a foreign netizen thought that everyone in Sichuan province has a giant panda at home and would walk it when going out. However, that's of course not the case in reality. What misconceptions did you have about China before you came here? And then how did you resolve those misunderstandings? Please share it with your peers.

（三）天空跑道——稻城亚丁

"一千个人眼里有一千个哈姆雷特"，一千个人眼里也有一千个稻城亚丁。有人说那是世界上最后一片净土，有人说去了就会累死、晕死、后悔死，还有人说去了后悔一天，不去后悔一辈子。那么这究竟是怎样一个地方呢？

稻城是指位于四川省甘孜藏族自治州的稻城县。这里靠近云南省的香格里拉，连接着泸沽湖和丽江。亚丁是指稻城县的亚丁自然保护区，主要由三座雪山和周围的河流、湖泊、高山草甸组成，是中国最原始、保存最完整的高山自然生态系统之一。

亚丁保护区最著名的景点是牛奶海和五花海。牛奶海其实是一座古冰川湖，终年被雪山环绕。湖泊的形状好像一个水滴，湖中碧蓝的雪水被一圈和牛奶一样的乳白色湖水环绕着，因此被称为牛奶海。这种景象大概是因湖底的石头反射太阳光而形成的。因为湖水的深度不一样，靠近岸边的湖水比较暗黑，越往深处看就越蓝得透亮。每当微风吹过，湖面如同宝石一样闪闪发光。五花海是亚丁海拔位置最高的湖。湖水清澈透亮，湖底则好像是黑

色的格子中填着浓浓淡淡的蓝色颜料。天气晴朗时,湖底的植物和湖水在阳光的照射下发出不同的光芒,而且不断变化。真的如同仙境一般!

牛奶海美景

那面对人间仙境,为什么还有人后悔呢?因为虽然有无敌美景,但是需要徒步5000米,而且是在海拔4000多米的地方活动,让游人感到十分辛苦。路途遥远的辛苦、危险的高原反应让很多游人半途而废,无功而返。但是也有勇敢者,就在这样的地方,一般人连走动都很困难,还敢全速奔跑!

从2016年开始,亚丁保护区每年都会举办"天空跑"(skyrunning)的比赛。这项比赛也是唯一一个在中国举办的天空跑世界系列赛积分赛。以"在天与地交接的地方奔跑"为口号,每年都有约200名越野跑选手参加比赛。比赛的"天空跑道"有2900米长,最高海拔是4700米。

虽然"天空跑道"一路穿越森林雪山,风景如画,但是面对极端条件,参赛者的身体和毅力都将受到严峻的考验。在历届比赛中,一位名叫四郎多吉的藏族小伙子堪称"黑马"[1]。他是亚丁本地人,在保护区管理处工作,从未接受过任何专业的越野跑

---

1 "黑马"比喻在比赛中突然出现的优秀选手。

第二眼看四川：向世界讲述四川故事
Second Glance at Sichuan: Telling Sichuan Stories to the World

训练，却能屡次在比赛中获得冠军。2019年，他又在超级转山的赛场获得冠军。冲过终点线，面对欢呼和掌声，四郎多吉先是双手合十，感谢所有在这里守候他的人，紧接着就双膝跪地，朝着正对面的亚丁三座神山深情而恭敬地叩拜了三次。他说神山带给藏族人信仰，保佑风调雨顺。他生长在这里，每年都去转山，感谢神山的赐予。不知道源自西方的天空跑原本有着怎样的含义，不过对中国人来说，在"天空跑道"的奔跑完全没有征服自然的意思，相反是要亲近自然，向自然献上人类的敬畏之心。

语言点例释

1. 因为湖水的深度不一样，靠近岸边的湖水比较暗黑，越往深处看就越蓝得透亮。

这句话的大意是"湖水在靠近岸边的地方比较黑，深处更蓝"。其中，"靠近"是动词，在这句话中的意思是"彼此的距离近"，例如"他家靠近一条河"。除了这个意思，"靠近"还有"接近，使距离缩小"的意思，例如"船慢慢地靠近岸边"。

2. 面对极端条件，参赛者的身体和毅力都将受到残酷的考验。

"将"是时间副词，用在动词前面作状语，多出现在书面语中，表示行为或情况不久以后就会发生，例如"明年我们将去国外交流学习"。

拓展阅读

高原反应

高原反应，也叫高原病、高山病，简称"高反"。人突然进入海拔3000米以上的地方后，会产生一些不舒服的感觉，例如头痛、失眠、疲倦、食欲减退、呼吸困难等。

读后思考

1. "牛奶海"名字的由来是什么？

2. 四郎多吉获得冠军后，双手合十，双膝跪地，朝着神山叩拜三次。他为什么会这样做？这是否与藏族人民的信仰有关系？

交流讨论

你喜欢户外运动吗？你觉得人们在户外运动中有哪些收获或乐趣？

(3) Daocheng Yading: Running Track to the Sky

As the saying goes: "There are a thousand Hamlets in a thousand people's eyes". Daocheng Yading also varies in people's eyes. Some people take it as the last pure land on this blue planet, some people joke that they are really dead tired, dizzy and regretful there, and others believe that one may regret for just one day by getting there, if not, will regret for a lifetime. So what kind of place is it?

The word "Daocheng" refers to Daocheng County in Ganzi Tibetan Autonomous Prefecture of Sichuan province close to Shangri-la of Yunnan province and neighbors Lugu Lake and Lijiang. And "Yading" refers to the Yading Nature Reserve in Daocheng County which is mainly composed of three snow mountains and the surrounding rivers, lakes, alpine grasslands and meadows. It is one of the most well-preserved and primitive alpine natural ecosystems in China.

The top attractions in Yading Nature Reserve are the Milk Lake and Five Color Lake. Milk Lake, from the Ice Age, is surrounded by snow mountains all year round and belted in milky white, naturally in the shape of a water drop. This phenomenon is likely formed by the reflection of sunlight off the stones at the bottom of the lake. Because of varying depths, the water shows dark blue near the lakeshore but much

brighter in deeper parts. Furthermore, when the breeze blows, the face of lake shimmers like a gem. As the highest lake in Yading, Five Color Lake is so crystal-clear that its bottom appears like a black palette filled with various shades of blue. The water plants at the bottom glow differently under the sun, even changing all the time. It's really like a fairyland!

But why do some people still regret being at this place? In spite of the stunning beauty, a lot of visitors feel exhausted because they have to hike 5,000 meters at an altitude of over 4,000 meters. Many of them give up halfway because of the long tough journey and dangerous altitude sickness. But for braver ones, they prefer running at full speed there though it's difficult for most people even to breathe.

Since 2016, the Skyrunning Festival has been held every year in Yading. This is also the only points race of Skyrunner World Series held in China. With the tagline "Running at the Edge of Sky and Earth", it attracts about 200 trail runners competing each year. The skyrunning route is 2,900 meters with the highest elevation of 4,700 meters.

Despite the picturesque route through forests and snowy mountains, the runners, facing hazardous circumstances, are greatly challenged both physically and mentally. In the past races, a young Tibetan man named Silang Duoji could indeed be called a "dark horse". As a local, he works for the reverse administrative office and has never had any professional training for trail running before, however, he has repeatedly won the championships. In 2019, he won the Yading ULTRA KORA. After crossing the finish line, greeted with cheers and applause,

Silang Duoji first thanked all that had waited for him with folded hands in praying posture. Then he knelt down on the ground and bowed three times toward the three holy mountains of Yading, with great respect. He said that the holy mountains bring Tibetan people faith and blessing. He grew up here and pays a visit to thank the holy mountains every year. Though it is uncertain about the meaning of the word "skyrunning" in western culture, Chinese people believe that it is definitely not to conquer nature, but to get close to and revere nature.

Notes

1. 因为湖水的深度不一样，靠近岸边的地方比较暗黑，越往深处看就越蓝得透亮。

　　This sentence basically means "湖水在靠近岸边的地方比较黑，深处更蓝"。Here, "靠近" is a verb which means "be close to". For example:

　　他家靠近一条河。

　　Besides this, "靠近" also means "to approach". For example:

　　船慢慢地靠近岸边。

2. 面对极端条件，参赛者的身体和毅力都将受到残酷的考验。

　　"将" is a time adverb and is always placed before a verb. "将" is often used in written language to indicate that an action or situation will occur in the near future. For example:

　　明年我们将去国外交流学习。

Extensive Reading

High Altitude Sickness

High altitude sickness is also known as altitude sickness and mountain sickness, or "高反 (gāofǎn)" in Chinese for short. It is a kind of discomfort caused by people's exposure to low pressure and low oxygen level when they enter a plateau at an altitude of more than 3,000 meters. Common symptoms of high altitude sickness include headache, insomnia, tiredness, loss of appetite, difficulty breathing, etc.

Questions

1. How did the Milk Lake get this name?

2. What do you think of Silang Duoji's actions, such as praying with folded hands, kneeling down on the ground and bowing toward the three holy mountains of Yading? What is the relationship between these postures and the belief of the Tibetans?

Discussion

Do you like outdoor activities? What are the achievements or pleasures that people can get from outdoor activities?

（四）守卫长江——诺水河水生动物自然保护区

2020年1月，一条突然的消息让中国人意外而又悲痛。科学家证实，"中国最大淡水鱼"长江白鲟已经灭绝。其实，科学家们认为早在2005—2010年，长江白鲟就已经灭绝了。除了白鲟，中国特有的中华鲟、长江鲟现在也被世界自然保护联盟（IUCN）评估为"极危"等级，就是有灭绝的危险。普通的中国人可能很难相信这一现实。在大家的心目中，长江一直是中国重要的水生生物宝库，是世界上水生生物种类最丰富的河流之一。但近年来，大家已强烈意识到必须更加积极地守卫长江。因此，2020年，中国开始实施长江十年禁渔计划。

四川位于长江上游，对整个长江的生态负有重大的责任。诺水河水生动物自然保护区的建立就是四川人民为守卫长江付出的努力之一。保护区位于四川省通江县，总面积为9220公顷[1]，主

1　1公顷=10 000平方米。

要保护对象为大鲵、水獭等珍稀水生动物及其生活的环境。这里大鲵的数量是全国最多的。大鲵是世界上体形最大的一种两栖动物，体长最长的可以达到2米，体重最大的有50公斤。它们可以用肺呼吸，但是肺的发育不完善，需要用湿润的皮肤来帮助呼吸，就好像青蛙一样。从进化论的观点来看，它们是从鱼类向陆地动物演化的一个环节。

大鲵

光雾山—诺水河国家地质公园正是在此保护区的基础上建立了起来。这个公园位于陕西和四川的交界处，距离成都390千米。公园里最震撼的景观是喀斯特地貌，包括地表和地下两种类型。地表有现在仍在生长发育的洞穴钙化瀑布、800平方米的数万根"鹅管"群、壮观的石盾群。这不仅在中国，而且在全世界也很罕见。地下的岩溶洞穴则是洞中有洞，洞与洞之间的通道还有很多变化，就好像迷宫一样。最令人惊喜的是，公园里已经发现的128个溶洞分布于寒武纪、奥陶纪、志留纪、二叠纪、三叠纪5个时代的地层中，是世界上发育于最多不同地质时代母岩的溶洞

第二眼看：
向世界讲述四川故事
Second Glance at Sichuan: Telling Sichuan Stories to the World

群。这样复杂的地层结构充分展示了地块33亿年的沧桑变化，是研究地球历史演变的最优秀样本。要知道33亿年也就比地球年轻10亿岁！在地层中，科学家们曾发现"蜀兽目"的动物化石，距今约1.5亿年，是世界上最古老的哺乳动物化石之一。

走出诺水河园区，来到光雾山园区，则是另外一番风景。这里的植被覆盖率达到98%，40万亩[1]的原始森林是各种珍贵植物的宝库，一同构成了四川北部的天然屏障。那么光雾山之名有何由来？这里的"光"字是四川方言，意思是"只有"，所以"光雾山"这个名字就是说这里只有雾，几乎看不到山。原来这座山的海拔2500米，气温很低，整座山都被云雾遮掩，很难见到太阳。光雾山地区流行一首山歌，里面唱道："哥在山中抓把雾，轻轻捏出数滴水；妹在山中唱支歌，甜得满山细雨飞。"你看，连情歌里面都充满了雾和雨呢！

光雾山还是中国秋景最迷人的地方之一。到了深秋，整座山成为红叶的海洋。说是红叶，可不只是红色一种。随着山势升高，红叶的颜色不断变化，蓝、绿、黄、橙红的叶子令人眼花缭乱。每年观赏红叶的时间足有一个月，先看树林五彩缤纷，再看树叶飘落，好像梦境。如果仔细看，你会发现树叶有手掌的形状、羽毛的形状等。这些美丽的颜色和形状在雾中不断变化，大概就是诗人说的"秋日更胜春光"了吧？

1　亩，中国常用的土地面积单位，1亩相当于666.67平方米。

语言点例释

1. 除了白鲟，中国特有的中华鲟、长江鲟现在也被世界自然保护联盟（IUCN）评估为"极危"等级，就是有灭绝的危险。

"评估"是一个动词，意思是"（对质量、水平、成绩等）进行评议或估价，分出好坏或等级"，例如"中介在评估房子的价值"。

2. 从进化论的观点来看，它们是从鱼类向陆地动物演化的一个环节。

"从……来看"表示从某一个方面、角度、观点出发讨论问题，例如"从他考试的成绩来看，他平时根本没有认真学习"。

拓展阅读

地质年代

地质学家和古生物学家根据地层自然形成的先后顺序，将地层分为5代12纪。在各个不同时期的地层里，大都保存有古代动、植物的标准化石。文中提到的寒武纪、奥陶纪、志留纪、二叠纪属于古生代，约开始于5.7亿年前，结束于2.5亿年前。而三叠纪属于中生代，约开始于2.5亿年前，结束于6500万年前。

读后思考

1. 请根据文章内容介绍大鲵这种动物。
2. "光雾山"里的"光"是什么意思？

交流讨论

请上网查找三种珍稀水生动物，说一说它们的外形特点、生活地区、现存数量以及人类是如何保护它们的。

珍稀水生动物	珍稀水生动物1	珍稀水生动物2	珍稀水生动物3
外形特点			
生活地区			
现存数量			
保护方法			
图片			

请联系你的国家环境保护的情况，谈一谈人类应该怎样与自然和谐相处。

(4) Nuoshuihe National Nature Reserve for Rare Aquatic Animals: Protection of Yangtze River

In January 2020, Chinese people were shocked and saddened by the sudden news that the Yangtze paddlefish, China's largest freshwater fish, has now been declared extinct by scientists. In fact, scientists believe that the Yangtze paddlefish was already extinct as early as sometime between 2005 and 2010. Apart from Yangtze paddlefish, the endemic species such as Chinese sturgeon and Dabry's sturgeon (also known as Yangtze sturgeon) are now listed by the International Union for Conservation of Nature (IUCN) as "critically endangered", meaning at risk of extinction. Many Chinese found this reality hard to accept. Yangtze River is widely regarded as a treasure house of the richest aquatic lives in both China and the world. But in recent years, people have become fully aware that more active safeguarding of Yangtze River is urgently needed. In 2020, the Chinese government began a 10-year fishing ban on the Yangtze River.

Sichuan, located in the upper reaches of the Yangtze River, shoulders great responsibility for the ecosystem of the entire river. The Nuoshuihe National Nature Reserve for Rare Aquatic Animals is one of the contributions made by Sichuan people to protect the Yangtze River. Situated in Tongjiang County of Sichuan province, the reserve covers a

total area of 9,220 hectares[1], aiming to protect rare aquatic animals such as giant salamanders and otters, as well as their living environment. This area gathers the largest population of giant salamanders in China. The giant salamander is the largest amphibian in the world, with a maximum body length of 2 meters and a maximum weight of 50 kilograms. It breathes with vestigial lungs, so it uses moist skin to exchange gas as an assisted form of breathing, which is just like a frog. From the evolutionary viewpoint, this occurs during the biological evolution from fish to terrestrial animals.

Based on this nature reverse, Guangwushan-Nuoshuihe National Geopark was established. The park is located on the border of Shaanxi and Sichuan provinces, 390 kilometers from Chengdu. The most striking view in the park is the karst landforms, both above ground and underground. On the ground, there are caves in which mineral formations are still growing, such as calcified waterfalls, stalactites shaped like thin goose feathers taking up 800 square meters, and groups of spectacular shield-shaped stalactites. These are rare sceneries not only in China, but in the world. Beneath the ground, karst caves are complex mazes of smaller caves and tunnels linking them. Most surprisingly, 128 karst caves found in the park are distributed in different stratigraphies of the Cambrian, Ordovician, Silurian, Permian, and Triassic Period, which is the world's largest group of karst caves in the geological era of parent rocks developing. Such complex geology has witnessed profound changes of this massif over 3.3 billion years and is the best research sample of the evolution of the earth, because the earth,

---

1 1 hectare = 10,000 square meters.

Second Glance at Sichuan: Telling Sichuan Stories to the World

after all, is only one billion years older than it. In the strata, scientists have discovered the fossil of "Shuotherium", dating back to about 150 million years ago, which is one of the world's oldest mammal fossils.

Entering Guangwushan park area, one will find a different picture. Here the vegetation coverage has reached 98%, and 400,000 mu^1 of primary forests is a treasure house of various precious plants, together acting as a natural boundary in northern Sichuan. Why is it called Guangwushan? The word "光 (guāng)" in Sichuan dialect means only and "雾 (wù)" means fog, hence the name "Guangwushan" means that there is only fog here so that the mountain is invisible. The mountain has an altitude of 2,500 meters with very low temperature, therefore the whole mountain is covered by clouds, even hardly to see the sun. It is said that there is a very popular folk song in this mountainous area, which says: "The boy grabbed the fog in the mountain to gently pinch out a few water drops; the girl sang a song in the mountain, which was so sweet that a drizzle fluttered." Even love songs are full of fog and rain!

Here, one can enjoy some of the most gorgeous autumn sceneries in China. In late autumn, the whole mountain becomes an ocean of red leaves. In spite of being called red leaves, the leaves are not just in red color. As the mountains rise, the color of red leaves changes constantly, with shades of dazzling blue, green, yellow and orange. The annual time for viewing red leaves is one month long, first to enjoy the colorful forests, and then to see the leaves falling like a dream. Only when near the mountain can one tell that the leaves have different shapes of palms,

---

1 *Mu* is a unit of land area (1 *mu* ≈ 666.67 square meters).

feathers and so on. These beautiful colors and shapes are constantly changing amongst the fog, which is probably like what a poet said: "Autumn is better than spring".

> ### Notes
>
> 1. 除了白鲟，中国特有的中华鲟、长江鲟现在也被世界自然保护联盟 (IUCN) 评估为"极危"等级，就是有灭绝的危险。
>
> "评估" is a verb that means "to estimate, to assess". For example: 中介在评估房子的价值。
>
> 2. 从进化论的观点来看，它们是从鱼类向陆地动物演化的一个环节。
>
> "从……来看" means to discuss the issue from a certain point of view. For example:
>
> 从他考试的成绩来看，他平时根本没有认真学习。

Extensive Reading

Geological Epochs

Geologists and paleontologists classify rock strata into five "eras" and twelve "periods" according to the natural sequence of strata formation. Fossils of ancient flora and fauna can usually be found within different periods of rock strata. The Cambrian, Ordovician, Silurian, and Permian period mentioned in the text belong to the Paleozoic Era, which began around 570 million years ago and ended around 250 million years ago. The Triassic period belongs to the Mesozoic Era, which began around 250 million years ago and ended around 65 million years ago.

Questions

What is the meaning of "光 (guāng)" in "光雾山 (Guāngwùshān)"?

Experience

Please find out three rare aquatic animals on the internet, and briefly sum up their appearance, living areas, existing numbers and human's protection approach.

第二眼看四川：
向世界讲述四川故事
Second Glance at Sichuan: Telling Sichuan Stories to the World

Rare Aquatic Animal	Rare Aquatic Animal 1	Rare Aquatic Animal 2	Rare Aquatic Animal 3
Appearance			
Living Areas			
Existing Number			
Protection Approaches			
Pictures			

 **Writing**

Based on the situation of environmental protection in your home country, please share your take on how human beings should live in harmony with nature.

三、民族篇

中国有56个民族,个性鲜明而又和谐相处,就好像一个大家庭中的56个兄弟姐妹。本篇为你讲述其中四个少数民族的个性与融合。

3. National Minorities

There are 56 ethnic groups in China, each with distinct characteristics yet all living in harmony, just like 56 brothers and sisters from one big family. This chapter focuses on the characteristics and integration of four ethnic minorities.

第二眼看四川：向世界讲述四川故事
Second Glance at Sichuan: Telling Sichuan Stories to the World

（一）云朵上的民族——羌族

四川省阿坝藏族羌族自治州是我国唯一的羌族聚居区。羌族是中国西部的一个古老的民族，对中国历史的发展和中华民族的形成有深远的影响。羌族的民族语言是羌语，20世纪80年代语言学家为羌语设计出了文字。由于羌族与汉族交往密切，所以很多羌族人都懂汉语。

还记得阿坝藏族羌族自治州吗？咱们讲九寨沟、卧龙保护区等美景的时候是不是就提到过这个地名？可以说，这里是四川乃至全中国风景最特别、最美丽的地方之一了！羌族人民自称"尔玛"或"尔咩"，意思是本地人。由于他们习惯把村寨和住房都建在山上，从下往上看这些房子就好像在云上一样，所以羌族也被称为"云朵上的民族"。

阿坝藏族羌族自治州美景

大部分羌族人信仰原始宗教，信奉多神和祖先。他们用白色的石英石作为神灵的象征，把这些石头崇敬地放在山中、林地、屋顶、室内等各个地方。例如，羌族人家的房顶一般都供有五块白石，分别象征天神、地神、山神、山神娘娘和树神。厨房里有

民族篇
National Minorities

一个三脚架,上面系着一个小铁环,代表火神。而负责祭祀这些神灵的祭师,羌语称"释比"或"许",在羌族社会中拥有崇高的地位。人们相信他能和神灵沟通,拥有神秘的力量。

如果想要亲身感受羌族文化的魅力,位于阿坝的桃坪羌寨绝对是一个很好的选择。这里距离成都139千米,是国家级重点文物保护单位。桃坪羌寨的设计完美地体现了羌族的建筑艺术:以一个古堡为中心,整个建筑群形成了8个放射形的部分,每个部分的出口都连着通道,最终构成一张大路网。在这张网中,本寨人能够自由来往,但外来的人却好像进入了迷宫。仔细看每栋房子,都是二到三层高,最下层是养牛羊的地方,上面为住房。房间里的地下供水系统最是独特:从高山上引来的泉水,经暗沟流到每栋房子,不仅可以调节室内温度,而且一旦有战争,还是最好的逃生暗道。你能想象吗?这样精巧的设计已经有2000多年的历史了!

来到这里你会发现,时间仿佛停止了。在寨子中,人们保留着最传统的生活习惯。采摘苹果的小孩子欢天喜地,穿着整齐民族服饰的老人慢慢经过,女人们一边织着羌绣一边聊天……真是好舒服的生活节奏!有的人家愿意接待游客,如果你走进这样的家庭,主人会给你端来香味扑鼻的羌家腊猪肉、各种各样的山野菜。如果你会喝酒,主人还会为你敬上醇香的青稞酒。这时,甜甜的祝酒歌唱起来,幸福的感觉让你终生难忘。

如果你去的时候正赶上过年或者过节,那就更热闹了!羌族最隆重的民族节日有"祭山会"和"羌年会",分别在四月初八和十月初一,也就是庆祝春天耕种和秋天收获的节日,充满了浓郁的宗教色彩。节日里,整个山寨的人都聚在一起,燃起熊熊的

第二眼看四川：向世界讲述四川故事
Second Glance at Sichuan: Telling Sichuan Stories to the World

篝火，吃着烤羊肉，喝着醇香的咂酒，唱山歌，跳锅庄，有时会热闹一整个晚上。

语言点例释

1. 人们都相信他能和神灵沟通，拥有神秘的力量。

   "沟通"是一个动词，意思是"使彼此的意见、思想、感情等相通"，例如"沟通思想，沟通中西文化"。

2. 在这张网中，本寨人能够自由来往，但外来的人却好像进入了迷宫。

   这句话的大意是"本寨人能自由通行，外来人却不能"。其中，"却"是一个关联副词，用在后面的分句中表示转折，例如"我来了，他却没来"。

桃坪羌寨

读后思考

1. 羌族为什么被大家称为"云朵上的民族"？
2. 请查阅与羌族文化相关的资料，谈一谈羌族文化的特点。

民族篇
National Minorities

🍃 交流讨论 🍃

很多民族都拥有自己独特的建筑形式，请介绍你的国家的一处充满个性的建筑，并说明这种建筑的功能以及与文化的关系。

建筑形式	功能	文化

(1) Qiang Ethnic Group: People Living on the Clouds

Aba Tibetan and Qiang Autonomous Prefecture in Sichuan province is the only concentrated residential area for the Qiang people in China. Qiang is an ancient ethnic group in western China, which has a profound influence on the development of Chinese history as well as the formation of the Chinese nation. Their native language is Qiang (or Chiang), for which linguists created a writing system in the 1980s. Qiang people have always been in close contact with Han people, so many of them can understand standard Chinese.

Does the place Aba Tibetan and Qiang Autonomous Prefecture sound familiar? It has been mentioned several times in the previous chapters about Jiuzhaigou, Wolong and other beautiful places. Aba is arguably one of the most special and beautiful places in Sichuan and even China! The Qiang people call themselves "尔玛 (ěrmǎ)" or "尔咩 (ěrmiē)", which means locals. They are also known as the "people living on the clouds", because they are used to building their villages and houses on the mountains, which look like being on the clouds from below.

Most Qiang people believe in primitive religion, worshiping multiple gods, as well as their ancestors. They take white quartz stones as a symbol of gods and place them respectfully in the mountains and woodlands, on the rooftops or indoors. For example, Qiang people usually place five white stones on their house roofs, respectively symbolizing the gods of heaven, earth, mountains and trees, as well as the goddess of mountains. In the kitchen, there is a three-legged stand with a small iron ring, representing the god of fire. The "priests" in charge of sacrificing for the gods, known as "Shibi" or "Xu" in Qiang language, hold a high position in Qiang society. It is believed that they can communicate with the gods and possess mystical powers.

Taoping Village in Aba is definitely a good choice to experience the charm of Qiang culture. 139 kilometers away from Chengdu, it is one of the key cultural heritage sites under national-level protection. The design of the Taoping Village perfectly reflects the architectural art of Qiang: centered on an ancient castle, the architectural complex consists of eight radial sections, each of which is connected to a passageway at the exit, forming a large network. In this network the locals can move freely, but for the outsiders it seems to enter a maze. Each house has two or three floors. The bottom floor is used for raising sheep and cattle, while the upper floors are for housing. The underground water supplies in the room are very unique: the spring water from high mountains flows to each house through the under drains, which can not only regulate the indoor temperature, but is also the best way to escape in case of war. Can you imagine that this ingenious design has been around for more

民族篇
National Minorities

than 2,000 years?

In this village, one may feel that time stands still, because the locals have maintained the most traditional living habits. Children picking apples happily, the seniors dressed in neat ethnic costumes passing by slowly, women making Qiang embroidery while chatting, what a comfortable pace of life! Some Qiang families are willing to receive tourists, who will be served with zesty Qiang cured pork and various wild vegetables, as well as the highland barley wine if needed. Meanwhile, sweet toasting songs will arise, and such feelings of happiness will be a once in a lifetime experience.

It will be more than lively and bustling during the Spring Festival or other holiday seasons. The most grand festivals of Qiang people include "祭山会 (Jìshānhuì)" and "羌年会 (Qiāngniánhuì)", respectively held on April 8th and October 1st on the Chinese lunar calendar, to celebrate spring farming and fall harvest, full of religious nature. During the festivals, all the villagers will gather up to light a roaring bonfire, eat roast mutton, drink the mellow "咂酒 (zājiǔ)" (a sort of liquor), sing folk songs and join the "锅庄 (guōzhuāng)" folk dance, sometimes for an entire night.

Notes

1. 人们都相信他能和神灵沟通，拥有神秘的力量。

"沟通" is a verb which means "to link up, to communicate". For example:

沟通思想、沟通中西文化

2. 在这张网中，本寨人能够自由来往，但外来的人却好像进入了迷宫。

This sentence basically means "本寨人能自由通行，外来人却不能"。Here, "却" is a correlative adverb used in the second clause to indicate comparison. For example:

我来了，他却没来。

Questions

1. Why are the Qiang people called the "people living on the clouds"?

2. Please look up for information about Qiang culture and sum up its characteristics.

Discussion

Many ethnic groups have their own unique architectural forms. Please introduce a distinctive architecture in your country and explain its function(s) and the relationship to the local culture.

Architectural Forms	Function(s)	Culture

（二）大山里的桃花源——纳西族古寨

东晋大诗人陶渊明写的《桃花源记》在中国可以说是家喻户晓。故事里有一个与世隔绝的村子，位于"桃花源"，也就是一片桃树林的源头。最早来到这里的人们是为了躲避战争，后来发现这里是一个很适合居住的地方，于是一住就是好几百年。因为从来不跟外面的世界联系，所以村子里始终保留着古老的风俗和自然的生活方式。从这个故事开始，中国人就把拥有理想生活而又与世隔绝的地方称为"桃花源"。当然，这个故事只是作者美好的想象，但是就在四川凉山的深处居然真有这样一个"桃花源"！这个古老的村子就是纳西族人民世世代代生活的俄亚古寨。

俄亚古寨在四川和云南的交界处，四周被重重的高山和河流环绕。通往古寨的道路崎岖坎坷，交通很不方便。正是由于这样封闭的自然环境，俄亚古寨至今仍保留着许多纳西族的古老风俗，被社会学家们称为"纳西族原生态文化留存地"和"社会活化石"。在纳西语中，"纳"的意思是"大""宏伟"，"西"指"人"。纳西族主要生活在云南省的丽江市和四川省的凉山。

俄亚古寨一共有200多户人家，每家的房屋靠山而立，连成了一片。房屋与房屋之间只留有窄窄的通道，大部分通道窄得一次只能通过一头牛。每家房屋有三层，最底层养牛羊，上面住人。最为特别的是，房屋的第三层彼此相通，从下往上形成一个整体，很像一个大蜂巢，显得十分壮观。这样的设计是为了更好地保护村民，抵抗外敌。因为对村民来说，万一有危险，可以迅速撤离到其他人家，但是对外来的敌人来说，这里就是一个大迷宫，进来容易，找到方向可就难了！

历史学家和社会学家们对俄亚古寨的源头有很多不同的猜测。有的学者认为，俄亚古寨是明朝时丽江木氏土司的"兵站"，村民则是当时在兵站的军队的后人。也有学者认为，俄亚古寨是明朝时丽江木氏土司的一个管家建立的。但不管怎么说，四百多年来几乎与世隔绝的历史和文化使俄亚古寨形成了一种独特的气

第二眼看四川：向世界讲述四川故事
Second Glance at Sichuan: Telling Sichuan Stories to the World

质和魅力。

如果你受到"桃花源"的召唤来到这里，一定要安静地做事，不要惊动古寨里的人们。因为寨子实在是太宁静了。这里的房子都不上锁，推开一扇木门，随着一声有些沉闷古老的"吱呀"声，就走进了一家，然后再走到下一家。你可以在任何一家面向大山敞开的阳台上小站一会儿，看对面的美好风光，看更远处的白云。还可以在任何一家小坐，喝一口清清的泉水，尝一杯甜甜的黄酒，吃一把香香的炒麦，然后离开，再走进下一家。古寨里的每条小巷，道上全是泥土，走进去，双脚就在泥土中行走，就像走进沙漠一样。当你的脚陷入这里的泥土，你会感觉自己自然而然地成了古寨的一部分。

语言点例释

1. 最早来到这里的人们是为了躲避战争，后来发现这里是一个很适合居住的地方，于是一住就是好几百年。

"……，于是……"可以用来表示承接，后一件事情紧接着前一件事情发生，例如"他不喜欢这个工作，于是离开了这家公司"。需要注意的是，"于是"后面的事情往往是由前一件事情引起的，例如"风停了，下起雨来，于是人们打起了雨伞"。

2. 历史学家和社会学家们对俄亚古寨的源头有很多不同的猜测。

"猜测"是一个动词，和"猜想"相近，意思是"根据某些现象做出估计、想象"。例如"这件事非常复杂，又没有线索，让人很难猜测"。

延伸阅读

陶渊明

东晋诗人，生活年代是公元352或365年到427年，擅长用平实的语言表达丰富的感情和深刻的思想，在中国文学史上有着崇高的地位。

民族篇
National Minorities

交流讨论

你的国家有哪些地方算得上是"桃花源"？请选择一个"桃花源"，完成下面的表格。

地名	国家	简要介绍	缘由	照片/图片/视频

记录写作

查阅与"桃花源"相关的资料，说一说什么样的地方算得上是"桃花源"。

(2) Naxi Ancient Village: Peach Blossom Spring Amongst the Mountains

"Peach Blossom Spring", written by Tao Yuanming, a great poet of the Eastern Jin Dynasty (317–420), is widely known in China. In this story, there is a secluded village located in the "peach blossom eden", the source of a peach forest. The first settlers were here to escape from wars, and later found it was a good place to live, where they have been staying for hundreds of years. Isolated from the world, people in this village have always kept their ancient customs and natural way of living. From this story on, such isolated land with an ideal life is called "Peach Blossom Spring" by Chinese people. Do you believe that such fictional land of beauty can be found in reality? That is the Eya ancient village in the Liangshan mountainous areas of Sichuan, where Naxi people have lived for generations.

Located in the border areas between Sichuan and Yunnan

provinces, the Eya village is surrounded by mountains and rivers. The road to the village is so rough and bumpy that transportation is rather underdeveloped. But it is because of such an enclosed natural environment that many ancient customs of Naxi ethnic group are still preserved in Eya village, which is described by sociologists as "Naxi Original Culture Preservation Area" and "a living monument to the society". In Naxi language, "Na" means big or magnificent, and "Xi" means people. Naxi ethnic group mainly live in Lijiang city of Yunnan province and Liangshan mountainous areas of Sichuan province.

In Eya village there are over 200 households, with their houses built at the foot of a mountain and interconnected into a whole. Only narrow lanes are left among the houses, most of which are so narrow that only one cow can pass at a time. Each house has three floors, with cattle and sheep at the bottom and people on the upper floors. The most special thing is that all the third floors of houses are connected to one another, becoming a whole from bottom to top, much like a huge beehive, very spectacular. This is designed to better protect the villagers against foreign aggressors. Because for the villagers, it is easy to evacuate to others' houses in case of danger, but for the aggressors, they would feel like getting caught in a big maze.

Different theories among historians and sociologists abound as to the origin of this ancient village. Some scholars believe that Eya village was the military depot belonging to Chieftain Mu of Lijiang in the Ming Dynasty, and the villagers were the descendants of the soldiers at the military depot then. While other scholars believe that this village was established by a housekeeper of Chieftain Mu. But one thing is for sure, the over four hundred years of isolated history and culture have shaped Eya village's unique character and charm.

Visitors must be quiet and not disturb the people inside the ancient village, because it is so tranquil here. The houses are all unlocked. Push open a wooden door with a dull and creaky sound, one can enter a house and then the next. One can look out of any balcony that faces the mountains, enjoying the beautiful scenery on the opposite side and the white clouds in the distance. Additionally, tourists can also visit any house they like, sipping the clear spring water, tasting a cup of sweet yellow rice wine, having a handful of fragrant fried wheats, and then leave and walk into the next house. Every lane in the village is covered with mud, walking in the mud is like walking in a desert. With the feet sinking into the mud here, one may feel naturally becoming a part of the village.

Notes

1. 最早来到这里的人们是为了躲避战争，后来发现这里是一个很适合居住的地方，于是一住就是好几百年。

"……，于是……" can be used to indicate successive relation. For example:

他不喜欢这个工作，于是离开了这家公司。

It is important to note that the event after "于是" is generally caused by the preceding events. For example:

风停了，下起雨来，于是人们打起了雨伞。

2. 历史学家和社会学家们对俄亚古寨的源头有很多不同的猜测。

"猜测" can be a noun or a verb which means "to guess, to conjecture", similar to "猜想". For example:

这件事非常复杂，又没有线索，让人很难猜测。

第二眼看四川：
向世界讲述四川故事
Second Glance at Sichuan: Telling Sichuan Stories to the World

❧ Extensive Reading ❧

Tao Yuanming

Tao Yuanming (352 or 365–427) was a Chinese poet of the Eastern Jin Dynasty, a master of expressing rich feelings and profound thoughts in plain language, occupying a lofty position in the history of Chinese literature.

❧ Discussion ❧

Name some places in your country or culture that might be regarded as "Peach Blossom Spring". Please select one of them and then complete the table below (with photos, pictures or videos).

Place	Country/Culture	Brief Introduction	Reasons	Photos, Pictures or Videos

❧ Writing ❧

Look up the information related to "Peach Blossom Spring", and explain what kind of place it is.

(三) 燃烧的狂欢节——彝族火把节

每年农历六月二十四日，彝族人民都会迎来自己最重要的传统节日——火把节。彝族是中国的第六大少数民族，居住在四川、云南、贵州等地。其中，四川凉山彝族自治州是最大的彝族聚居区。凉山州在四川省的西南部，是四川民族类别和少数民族人口最多的地区，而且是古代"南方丝绸之路"的必经之地。这里海拔1500米左右，冬暖夏凉，四季如春，天空洁净清朗。州府西昌市，天上总是挂着一轮明亮而皎洁的月亮，有"月城"之称。

关于火把节的由来，有很多种说法，不过据历史学家研究，节日最初应该与彝族人民对火的信仰有关。因为火把节在彝语中被称为"都则",意思就是"祭火"。学者们认为,人们过火把节最初应该是希望用火来驱除害虫,保护庄稼。事实上,在整个彝族文化中,对火的祭祀非常普遍。有的地方,家庭主妇们会在每年的农历正月初一和六月二十四,选一块最肥的肉扔进燃烧的火塘,祈祷火神护佑平安;有的地方则会在正月初二或初三开"火神会"。在每个彝族家庭,做饭取暖的火塘都会被看作火神居住的神圣之地,绝对禁止用脚踩或者跨过去。

火把节

到了晚上,各村寨都用干松木和松明子扎成大火把竖立在寨中,各家门前也都会竖起小火把。所有火把点燃以后就是一片火海。人们拿着小的火把成群结队地行走在村边和山间,把火把插在农田中间。远远望去,人群的队伍好像一条条巨大的火龙,十分壮观。最后大家还会汇聚到广场,把小的火把堆成火塔,唱歌跳舞,整夜都不休息。

火把节一般会进行三天三夜。第一天是迎火。这一天,家家

第二眼看四川：
向世界讲述四川故事
Second Glance at Sichuan: Telling Sichuan Stories to the World

户户宰杀牛、羊和猪，用酒肉迎接火神。出门在外的人们都要赶回家吃团圆饭，全家人一起用火把照遍屋里的每个角落。第二天是赞火，也是火把节的高潮。一大早，男女老少都会穿上节日的盛装，带上煮熟的坨坨肉、荞馍，聚集在祭台圣火下，参加各式各样的传统活动，例如赛马、摔跤、唱歌、选美。当傍晚来临时，成千上万的人举着火把从四面八方涌向同一个地方，烧红天空。人们围着篝火尽情地跳啊唱啊，直到深夜。当篝火就要熄灭的时候，一对对谈恋爱的男女会悄悄走进山坡或者树丛，弹着琴享受爱情的甜蜜。火把节的第三天叫送火。人们搭设祭火台，举行送火仪式，请求火神赐给大家安康和幸福。这时大家还要带着第一天宰杀的鸡的羽毛来一起烧掉，象征着邪恶的病魔和瘟神被消灭了。

　　火把节上有一个特别重要也是大家最喜欢的节目——选美。评委由民间的德高望重的老人组成，按照彝族传统的审美观选出最好看的男女青年。参赛的女孩子们穿着美丽的传统长裙，身上的银饰叮当作响。在彝族人看来，美女一定要头发浓，眼睛大，鼻梁高，脖子长，皮肤细腻红润，身材不胖不瘦。参赛的男孩子们则梳着传统的发型，带着特别的腰带和宝剑，牵着骏马，一个个仪表堂堂、勇敢雄健。除了外表，不管男女，才华更加重要。老人们会参考大家的意见，全面评价选手们的言谈举止、人品性格等。

民族篇
National Minorities

🍃 语言点例释 🍃

1. 关于火把节的由来，有很多种说法，不过据历史学家研究，节日最初应该与彝族人民对火的信仰有关。

"据"在这句话中是一个介词，意思是"按照，依据"，可以用来引出凭借、依据，例如"据专家介绍，这个信息并不准确"。

2. 当篝火就要熄灭的时候，一对对谈恋爱的男女会悄悄走进山坡或者树丛，弹着琴享受爱情的甜蜜……

"享受"是一个动词，意思是"在心理上或生活上得到满足，要求和愿望得以实现"，例如"中国人在春节都会回家过年，享受家的温暖"。

🍃 延伸阅读 🍃

南方丝绸之路

"南方丝绸之路"又叫"蜀身毒道"（"蜀"指四川，"身毒"指古代的印度）。这条道路从四川成都开始，经过云南进入缅甸，最后到达印度。通过这条道路，中原的人们把蜀布、丝绸、茶叶等物品卖出去，再运回玉器、宝石、香料等。于是，中国与西南亚及欧洲的经济、文化、政治、民族交流就在这条路上发展起来。

🍃 读后思考 🍃

1. 火把节的起源是什么？

2. 火把节一般有几天？分别有什么活动？

🍃 交流讨论 🍃

1. 在你们国家或民族文化中，有没有对"火"的信仰和祭祀？如果有，和彝族的火把节相比有哪些相同点和不同点？

2. 请根据网上查到的资料，总结一下彝族人民传统的审美观，在你看来，这和中国当代年轻人的审美观相比有哪些相同点和不同点？

Second Glance at Sichuan: Telling Sichuan Stories to the World

(3) Burning Carnival: Torch Festival of Yi Ethnic Group

On the 24th day of the sixth lunar month every year, the Yi ethnic group celebrate their most important traditional festival, known as the Torch Festival. The Yi people are the sixth largest ethnic minority in China and reside in regions such as Sichuan, Yunnan, and Guizhou. Among them, Liangshan Yi Autonomous Prefecture in Sichuan is the largest settlement area for Yi people, which is located in the southwest of Sichuan, with the most diverse ethnic groups and the largest population of minorities in this province. It was also a crucial passage along the ancient "Southern Silk Road". It has an altitude of about 1,500 meters, characterized by mild winters, cool summers, and a spring-like climate throughout the year, with clear and pristine skies. The capital city of Liangshan Yi Autonomous Prefecture is Xichang, which is often adorned with a bright and shining moon at night, earning it the nickname "Moon City".

There are various interpretations regarding the origin of the Torch Festival, but according to historical research by scholars, the festival is believed to be closely related to the Yi people's worship of fire . In the Yi language, the Torch Festival is referred to as "都则 (dūzé)", which means "fire sacrifice". Scholars believe that the Torch Festival was originally intended to use fire to drive away pests and protect people's crops. In fact, the worship and sacrifice of fire are widespread in Yi culture. In some places, housewives would throw the fattest piece of meat into a burning fireplace on Lunar New Year and on the 24th day of the sixth lunar month to pray for the fire god's protection. In other

areas, Fire God Assembly is held on the second or third day of the lunar new year. In every Yi family, the fireplace for cooking and heating is considered as a sacred place where the fire god lives, and is strictly forbidden to be stepped on or crossed over.

On the evening of the Torch Festival, each village erects huge torches with dried pine wood and smaller torches in front of every house. All the lit torches create a sea of fire. People then gather in groups, holding small torches, and walk along the village outskirts and mountainsides. They insert the torches into the fields. From a distance, the procession of people resembles a massive fire dragon, creating a spectacular sight. Finally, everyone gathers in the central square, stacking the small torches into a tower of fire, singing, dancing and celebrating throughout the night without resting.

The Torch Festival typically lasts three days and three nights. The first day is to welcome the fire, when every family slaughters cattle, goats and pigs as offerings together with liquor to greet the fire god. During this time, people away from home rush back to join a family reunion dinner, using torches to illuminate every corner of the house. The second day is to praise the fire, representing the climax of the Torch Festival. Early in the morning, people of all ages dress in festive attire and gather under the sacred fire altar. They bring cooked chunks of meat and buckwheat bread, and participate in a variety of traditional activities, such as horse racing, wrestling, singing and beauty pageant. As evening approaches, thousands of people holding torches converge from all directions, and gather in one place, forming countless bonfires

that light up the sky. People sing and dance around the bonfires until late at night. When the bonfires are about to die out, couples in love quietly slip away into the hills or bushes, playing lutes and enjoying their sweet love. The third day is to send off the fire. On that day, people set up a fire altar and conduct a ceremony, praying to the fire god for health and happiness. They also need to burn the feathers of chickens slaughtered on the first day, symbolizing the eradication of the evil spirits of disease and plague.

The Torch Festival features a highly important and popular event known as the beauty pageant. The judging panel consists of respected elders from the community, selects the most attractive young men and women based on the traditional aesthetic standards of Yi ethnic group. The participating girls wear beautiful traditional long dresses adorned with tinkling silver accessories. According to the Yi people's perception of beauty, a beautiful girl must have thick hair, large eyes, a high nose bridge, a long neck, smooth and rosy skin, and a well-proportioned figure. The participating boys groom themselves in traditional hairstyles, wear special belts, carry swords, and hold the reins of spirited horses, presenting themselves as dignified, brave, and strong individuals. In addition to good looks, talent is more than appreciated. To make a comprehensive judgement, the judges evaluate the contestants' speeches, manners, personalities and other aspects based on the opinions of the community.

Notes

1. 关于火把节的由来，有很多种说法，不过据历史学家研究，节日最初应该与彝族人民对火的崇拜有关。

   In this case, "据" is a preposition which means "according to, in terms of". For example:

   据专家介绍，这个信息并不准确。

2. 当篝火就要熄灭的时候，一对对谈恋爱的男女会悄悄走进山坡或者树丛，弹着琴享受爱情的甜蜜……

   "享受" is a verb which means "to enjoy, to live it up". For example:

   中国人在春节都会回家过年，享受家的温暖。

Extensive Reading

Ancient Southern Silk Road

The ancient "Southern Silk Road", also known as the "Shu-Sindhu Road" ("Shu" refers to Sichuan province, and "Sindhu" refers to ancient India), used to be a trade route starting from Chengdu, passing through Yunnan province and entering Myanmar before finally reaching India. Along this route, people from Ancient China sold Sichuan silk, tea, and other goods and exchanged them for jade, gems, spices, and more. As a result, economic, cultural, political, and ethnic exchanges between China and Southwest Asia as well as Europe flourished along this road.

Questions

1. What is the origin of the Torch Festival?

2. Please summarize the traditional aesthetic values of the Yi ethnic group. In your opinion, what are the similarities and differences between their aesthetic values and those of contemporary young people in China?

（四）各民族一家亲——川西康巴文化

川西有中国第二大藏族聚居地。这里是长江和黄河的源头，拥有森林、雪山、冰川、峡谷、草原等众多美丽景观。自古以来，这里就是内地与西藏联系的重要通道，被称为"汉藏走廊"。同时，这里也是康巴文化的核心地区。

什么是康巴文化呢？"康"在藏语中是"边疆地区"的意思，"巴"在藏语中是"人"的意思。因此，"康巴"指的就是住在边缘地区的藏族人。原来，藏族人民在传统上认为拉萨是藏族地区的中心，把拉萨周围大部分地方称为"卫藏"，把西藏北部和青海境内大部分地区称为"安多"，而把更远一点的地方，包括西藏的昌都地区、青海玉树州、四川甘孜州和阿坝州的广阔地区称为"康"或"康巴"。据说，以前藏区流传这样一句话："卫藏的法，安多的马，康巴的人"，这句话说明了三个地区的特点。所谓"康巴的人"是夸奖康巴人聪明而顽强，勇敢有力量。历史上，清朝政府对西藏的政策一直有一个关键点，叫作"治藏必先安康"。这句话的意思是说，要治理好藏区，必须先治理好康巴。为什么有这样一个关键点呢？一来是因为康巴地区的战略地位很重要，是中国五大藏区的结合部分和交通中心，二来也是因为康巴文化对整个藏族文化的影响很大。

在川西，藏、汉、羌、彝、回、纳西6个民族世世代代共同生活，总人口超过200万，其中藏族占64%。不同的民族在这里真诚合作，亲密交往，就像一个和谐的大家庭。可以说，这里的民族关系是中华民族一家亲的最好体现。这种和睦的关系体现在文化上，就表现为多样性、兼容性、多重性和开放性等特点。

如果比较拉萨的建筑和甘孜地区的建筑，你会发现后者融合了藏族和汉族建筑艺术的特点。例如，藏式传统民居的屋顶都是平顶，但是甘孜的民居则增加了汉式人字形屋顶来防止雨水渗漏。房内，传统的藏式布局一定有一个独木楼梯。这种楼梯一来比较容易移动，可以有很多功能；二来形式独特，有装饰作用。但是也有缺点，这样的楼梯对老年人、小孩子和需要拿重东西的人来说就有点不太方便。于是甘孜地区的许多民居就借鉴了汉式宽大的楼梯，还加上扶手，既宽敞又方便。这是由于在这里，不同民族通婚的情况并不少见，所以很多家庭都享受着不同文化交汇的日常生活。例如，有的人家既吃大米、蔬菜，又吃传统的藏餐糌粑、牛肉；既过藏历春节，也过汉族的中秋节；既供着藏传佛教的佛像，又贴着新春民俗的对联。

在这样的文化氛围中，"康巴汉子"的形象越来越鲜明。康巴的男人们多身体健壮，习惯在高山深水中劳作，养成了吃苦耐劳的性格。在战争中，他们从来不害怕强大的敌人，赢得"康巴斗士"的美名；在日常生活中，他们擅长商业，出现了很多著名的商人。

语言点例释

1. 这种楼梯一来比较容易移动，可以有很多功能；二来形式独特，有装饰作用。

　　"装饰"是一个动词，意思是"在身体或物体的表面加些辅助的东西，使之更美观"，例如"他们在用彩灯装饰圣诞树"。除此之外，"装饰"还可以是名词，意思是"起修饰美化作用的物品"，例如"新家的各种装饰都很好看"。

2. 有的人家既吃大米、蔬菜，又吃传统的藏餐糌粑、牛肉；既过藏历春节，也过汉族的中秋节；既供着藏传佛教的佛像，又贴着新春民俗的对联。

　　"既……，又/也……"表示并列，各分句分别叙述或描写几件有联系的事情、几种情况或同一事物的几个方面，例如"这件新衣服既好看，又暖和"；"他既是我们的老师，也是我们的朋友"。

第二眼看四川：
向世界讲述四川故事
Second Glance at Sichuan: Telling Sichuan Stories to the World

读后思考

1. "康巴"指的是哪片地区？那里的文化有什么特点？
2. 川西各民族人民的关系如何？

亲身体验

成都武侯区有一条"藏族街"，充满藏族特色的建筑、门牌上的藏文、藏餐厅里的美食以及街上人们穿的民族服饰都会让你感受到浓浓的藏族风情。

(4) Kham Culture in Western Sichuan: All Ethnic Groups, One Happy Family

The Western Sichuan has the second largest settlement area of the Tibetan ethnic group in China. Located by the headwaters of the Yangtze River and the Yellow River, it boasts numerous beautiful landscapes, including forests, snow-capped mountains, glaciers, canyons, grasslands. Since ancient times, this area has served as an important passage connecting Xizang and other parts of China, known as the Han-Zang Corridor, and it is also the core of Kangba Culture.

So, what is the Kangba Culture? In the Tibetan language, "kang" means border areas and "ba" means people. Therefore, "Kangba" refers to Tibetans living in the peripheral areas. Traditionally, Tibetans considered Lhasa as the center of Tibetan areas, referring to the most places around Lhasa as "卫藏 (wèizàng)" (literally means "defense of Xizang"), and the northern Xizang as well as most of Qinghai-Tibetan regions as "安多 (ānduō)". The more distant

regions, including Changdu areas in Xizang, Yushu Prefecture in Qinghai, Ganzi Tibetan Autonomous Prefecture and Aba Tibetan and Qiang Autonomous Prefecture in Sichuan, were called "Kang" or "Kangba". Legend has it that there was a popular saying in Tibetan areas, "卫藏" (wèizàng) is well-known for its law, "安多" is well-known for its horses, and Kangba is well-known for its people", which highlights the characteristics of the three regions. The so-called "Kangba people" is a praise for the intelligence, tenacity, courage and strength of the locals. In history, the Qing government had issued a key policy regarding Xizang based on the idea that "To stabilize Kangba is the first step to effectively govern Xizang". One reason for this policy was the strategic importance of Kangba region, serving as a junction and transportation hub for the five major Tibetan areas of China, and the other reason was that Kangba Culture had a significant influence on Tibetan Culture as a whole.

In Western Sichuan, six ethnic groups—Tibetan, Han, Qiang, Yi, Hui, and Naxi—have been living together for generations, with the total population of over 2 million, of which Tibetans account for 64%. Here, different ethnic groups sincerely cooperate and closely interact with one another, just like a harmonious big family. It can be said that the ethnic relations here are the best reflection of the unity of all Chinese ethnic groups. Such kind of harmonious relationship is manifested culturally through characteristics such as diversity, inclusiveness, multiplicity, and openness.

Comparing the architectural style of Lhasa with that of Ganzi, one

may find that the latter incorporates both Tibetan and Han architectural elements. For example, while traditional Tibetan houses in Lhasa typically have flat roofs, the houses in Ganzi have added Han-style sloping roofs to prevent rainwater from seeping into the rooms. Inside the houses, the traditional Tibetan layout always includes a single wooden staircase, which is easier to move to serve other functions and presents unique decorative features. However, these staircases can also be somewhat inconvenient for the elderly, children, or individuals who need to carry heavy objects. Consequently, many houses in this region have adopted the wider and more convenient Han-style staircases with handrails. Since it is quite common for people of different ethnic groups to get married in this area, many families enjoy the daily life of cultural fusion. For instance, some families consume rice and vegetables, as well as traditional Tibetan dishes like Zanba (roasted highland barley flour) and beef. They celebrate not only the Tibetan New Year but also the Moon Festival of Han ethnic group. They may have Tibetan Buddhist statues in their homes while also displaying Spring Festival couplets from Han Chinese customs.

Under such cultural context, the image of "Kangba men" is becoming increasingly distinct. They are known for their robust physique and being accustomed to laboring in high mountains and deep waters, who have developed a character of endurance and hard work. In times of war, they were never afraid of the powerful enemies, and won the reputation of "Kangba fighters"; while in everyday life, they excel in business and have achieved success as many renowned businessmen.

民族篇
National Minorities

ᓚᓕ Notes ᓕᓚ

1. 这种楼梯一来比较容易移动，可以有很多功能；二来形式独特，有装饰作用。

"装饰" is a verb which means "to decorate". For example:

他们在用彩灯装饰圣诞树。

Besides, "装饰" can also be used as a noun, meaning "ornament, decoration". For example:

新家的各种装饰都很好看。

2. 有的人家既吃大米、蔬菜，又吃传统的藏餐糌粑、牛肉；既过藏历春节，也过汉族的中秋节；既供着藏传佛教的佛像，又贴着新春民俗的对联。

"既……，又/也……" indicates coordinate relation, or the simultaneous existence of several cases, properties or actions. For example:

这件新衣服既好看，又暖和。

他既是我们的老师，也是我们的朋友。

ᓚᓕ Questions ᓕᓚ

1. What region does "Kangba" refer to? What are the characteristics of the culture there?

2. How is the relationship among the various ethnic groups in the Western Sichuan? Which part of the article can provide insights?

ᓚᓕ Experience ᓕᓚ

In Chengdu's Wuhou District, there is a "Tibetan Street" filled with Tibetan-style buildings, Tibetan script on house plaques, delicious Tibetan cuisine in restaurants, and people wearing ethnic costumes on the street. All these elements will immerse you in rich Tibetan atmosphere.

四、历史篇

一段是没有留下文字的远古回忆，一段是用最精彩文字写成的历史传奇。有没有文字，都同样引人入胜，本篇为你讲述四川历史上的"高光时刻"。

 **4. History**

One is the ancient memory restored without words, and the other is the historical legend written in the most wonderful words. With or without words, the highlights of Sichuan's history in this chapter are extremely fascinating.

第二眼看四川：向世界讲述四川故事
Second Glance at Sichuan: Telling Sichuan Stories to the World

（一）灿烂三星堆

古蜀文明，是指从远古时期到春秋时期早期在四川地区产生和发展的古代文明。古蜀文明与华夏文明、良渚文明一起被称为中国上古三大文明。由于年代久远，对于古蜀文明，现在仍然有太多没有解开的谜团。因此当中国人谈到古蜀时，总是会用"神秘"来形容。不过，随着近年来考古发掘和历史研究的持续开展，古蜀文明的神秘面纱正在被慢慢揭开。其中最引人注目的就是"三星堆文化"。

如果你对古代文明感兴趣，那么到了四川一定不能错过位于四川广汉市的"三星堆博物馆"。博物馆位于三星堆遗址的东北角。据历史学家考证，整个三星堆遗址大约有12平方千米，距今约4500年至2900年。博物馆中陈列着大量出土文物，其中最引人注目的是一棵大铜树和一座大型青铜雕像。树和人的形体非常高大，外形奇特，和大家熟悉的中原文化出土文物差别很大。其实，如果你在博物馆认真参观，仔细听一听讲解，你会发现三星堆文化与中原文化有着密切的联系，但又有明显的个性，这也是许多人觉得古蜀文化特别神秘的一大原因。

三星堆的青铜雕像

除了研究三星堆文化与中原文化的联系与区别，很多历史学家还一直致力研究三星堆文化与中亚、古印度等文明的交往史。例如，三星堆博物馆中陈列的黄金面具和黄金手杖，在中国其他地区的考古文化中极为少见，会让人想起古埃及的黄金面罩和黄金权杖。再如人们一般认为，中华文明最推崇的应该是玉，俗话说"黄金有价，玉无价"，意思就是黄金至少还有价格，美玉却是无论多少钱也买不到的，但是在三星堆文化中，黄金却占有重要的地位。这些意外的联系让人不禁想到，三星堆文明是否与中华文明以外的文明有交往呢？

直到现在，有的人还以为古代四川由于地处内陆，很难与外界联系，因此四川文化是比较封闭的文化。其实这种想法大错特错，从三星堆文化就能看到，四川文化从一开始就与外界有着丰富的联系，而且在漫长的历史中，始终保持着开放的态度。

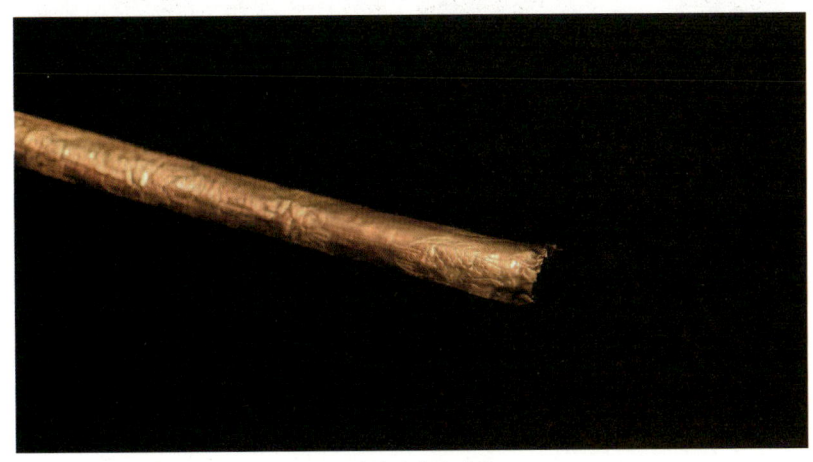

三星堆的黄金手杖

第二眼看四川：向世界讲述四川故事

Second Glance at Sichuan: Telling Sichuan Stories to the World

语言点例释

1. 由于年代久远，对于古蜀文明，现在仍然有太多没有解开的谜团。

"对于"是一个介词，可以用来引进动作、行为的对象，例如"对于有困难的人，我们应该帮助他们"。除此之外，"对于"还可以引出观察、评价问题的出发点、角度，例如"心情愉悦对于老年人的健康十分重要"。

2. 树和人的形体非常高大，外形奇特，和大家熟悉的中原文化差别很大。

"熟悉"是一个动词，意思是"（对人或事）了解得很清楚"，例如"他来成都十年了，很熟悉成都的情况"；"我们彼此都很熟悉"。

延伸阅读

三星堆黄金面具"撞脸"古埃及法老黄金面罩

比较下面的两个黄金面具，是不是觉得有几分相似？只不过三星堆的黄金面具是覆盖在青铜人像脸上的，而古埃及的黄金面罩则是罩在法老脸上的。

读后思考

1. 在许多人看来，古蜀文明为什么显得非常神秘？

2. 为什么说"从三星堆文化就能看出，四川文化从一开始就与外界有着丰富的联系"？

亲身体验

请在三星堆博物馆或者官方网站上找到一件你最感兴趣的文物，了解文物背后的故事，并说明你为什么特别感兴趣。

(1) Glorious Sanxingdui

Ancient Shu Civilization refers to the ancient civilization that emerged and developed in Sichuan region from ancient times to the early Spring and Autumn Period. Ancient Shu Civilization, along with Huaxia Civilization and Liangzhu Civilization, is known as one of the three great ancient civilizations of China. Because of its time-honored origins, there are still a lot of unsolved mysteries surrounding Ancient Shu Civilization. So when Chinese people speak of the Ancient Shu, they tend to describe it as "mysterious". In recent years, continued archaeological excavations and historical studies have begun to unveil the long-shrouded mysteries of the ancient Shu civilization. One of the most fascinating revelations is the Sanxingdui culture.

If one is interested in ancient civilizations, then a visit to the Sanxingdui Museum in the city of Guanghan is a must. It is located in the northeast of the Sanxingdui site. Covering an area of approximately 12 square kilometers, the entire Sanxingdui site, according to historical research, dates back 4500 to 2900 years ago. A lot of unearthed relics were displayed in the museum, the most striking of which are a large bronze tree and an upright bronze figure. Both of them are remarkably tall and possess unique features that differ greatly from the widely known Central Plains Culture. In fact, by listening to the tour guide carefully in the museum, visitors will find that the Sanxingdui Culture is closely related to the Central Plains Culture, but with distinct characteristics. This is one of the main reasons why the Ancient Shu Culture is perceived as particularly mysterious by many people.

向世界讲述四川故事
Second Glance at Sichuan: Telling Sichuan Stories to the World

In addition to the studies focusing on the connections and differences between the Sanxingdui Culture and the Chinese Central Plains Culture, many historians have been devoting to surveying the interactions between the Sanxingdui Culture and the civilizations in Central Asia, ancient India, and other regions. For instance, the golden masks and golden canes displayed in Sanxingdui Museum are rare in the cultures of other parts of China, but they may immediately remind people of those of ancient Egypt. Similarly, it is generally believed that the material most worshiped in the Chinese civilization is jade, as the saying goes, "gold has a price while jade is priceless", meaning that beautiful jade cannot be bought at any price. However, in the Sanxingdui Culture, gold holds a much more important position. Such unexpected connections make people wonder if the Sanxingdui Culture had interactions with some foreign civilizations beyond the Chinese civilization.

Until now, some people still believe that ancient Sichuan, due to its inland location, had limited contact with the outside world, and therefore its culture was rather closed-off. But this kind of assumption cannot be more misleading. From the Sanxingdui Culture, it's easy to figure out that Sichuan culture had rich connections with the outside world from the very beginning, and has always been open throughout its long history.

Notes

1. 由于年代久远，对于古蜀文明，现在仍然有太多没有解开的谜团。

"对于" is a preposition used to introduce the specific object of an action. For example:

对于有困难的人，我们应该帮助他们。

Besides this, "对于" can also introduce the speaker's attitude, viewpoint, and evaluation. It is similar to phrases like "with regard to" or "concerning". For example:

心情愉悦对于老年人的健康十分重要。

2. 树和人的形体非常高大，外形奇特，和大家熟悉的中原文化差别很大。

"熟悉" is a verb which means "to be familiar with, to have an intimate knowledge of". For example:

他来成都十年了，很熟悉成都的情况。

我们彼此都很熟悉。

Extensive Reading

Look-Alike Golden Masks

Do you find the following two masks somewhat similar? The golden mask of the Sanxingdui Culture covered the bronze figure's face, while the golden mask of ancient Egypt was placed on the Pharaoh's face.

Questions

1. For many people, why does the Ancient Shu Civilization seem to be so mysterious?

2. Why is it said that Sanxingdui culture reveals Sichuan's deep

Second Glance at Sichuan: Telling Sichuan Stories to the World

connections with the outside world from the very start?

Experience

Please find a piece of relics that interests you most in the Sanxingdui Museum or on its official website, and learn about the story behind the cultural relic. Then please explain why you are particularly interested in it.

（二）浪漫金沙

令人惊讶的是，灿烂的三星堆文化到了距今约 3200 年的时候突然发生了巨大的变化，城市也被废弃了。从出土的文物来看，一些带有明显的三星堆特色的陶器不见了，而另一些从来没有出现过的东西例如"龟甲占卜"[1]却突然出现。再后来，三星堆文化似乎就消失了。她为什么会消失？是因为有外来的敌人还是本身社会发生了变化？直到现在，历史学家们也没能给出明确的答案。

不过令人兴奋的是，历史学家们虽然没有回答三星堆文化为什么消失，但是找到了三星堆文化的后续文化，即金沙文化。

金沙文化的遗址就在今天的成都市青羊区。在这片遗址上，现在建有金沙遗址博物馆。博物馆的建筑非常有特色，采用了斜坡样式，象征着金沙文化慢慢升起。其中，我们在圆形的遗迹馆中能够看到古代的遗迹，而在方形的陈列馆则可以看到出土的文物。这两座建筑一圆一方，象征着中国古人"天圆地方"的观念，如今已经成为成都市的地标。

---

1 古人用乌龟的壳来预测未来的一种方法。

历史篇 History

金沙博物馆

我们在金沙遗址博物馆中能够看到很多藏品都与三星堆博物馆中的十分相似，例如黄金面具、石跪人像。但有趣的是，这些藏品比三星堆博物馆中的要小得多。有历史学家分析说，金沙时期的社会生产力可能比三星堆时期要差得多，所以很难再造出像铜树和铜像那样大型的器物。

在金沙遗址博物馆的中心位置，我们可以看到一件"镇馆之宝"，也就是整个博物馆中最珍贵的一件文物——"太阳神鸟金饰"。这件金饰外径12.5厘米，厚0.02厘米，重20克。整个图案好像一幅剪纸画，线条简练流畅，充满动感。内层图案为顺时针旋转的十二道太阳光芒，外层图案则是逆时针飞翔的四只小鸟。有历史学家认为，十二道光芒象征一年的十二个月，而四只小鸟则象征一年的四个季节，暗示时光的流逝。中国古人说"光阴似箭"，当代流行歌曲则唱道"我的青春小鸟一去不返"。这些浪漫的比喻在金沙文化的"太阳神鸟金饰"中得到了生动的体现。

正因为此，四川人十分喜欢太阳神鸟的图案，把它定为成都

第二眼看四川：向世界讲述四川故事

Second Glance at Sichuan: Telling Sichuan Stories to the World

市的城市标志，用在了各个地方。在成都，我们会在公交车站牌上或城市宣传画上见到这个标志。事实上，不光四川人喜欢，这个图案在2005年还被国家文物局公布确认为中国文化遗产标志。

语言点例释

1. 再后来，三星堆文化似乎就消失了。

"似乎"是一个副词，与作为副词时的"仿佛、好像"意思相近，可以表示不十分肯定，不一定是事实，例如"我似乎在什么地方见过他""三天不见，似乎离别了三年"。除此之外，"似乎"还可以用于表达商量，例如"这件事咱们似乎可以不用管"；"这么贵的东西似乎不应该买"。

2. 有历史学家分析说，金沙时期的社会生产力可能比三星堆时期要差得多，所以很难再造出像铜树和铜像那样大型的器物。

"分析"是一个动词，意思是"把事物分成若干部分，分别进行观察、研究，发现它们各自的特点和彼此的关系"，例如"她分析出失败的原因后找到了解决的方法"。

延伸阅读

天圆地方

"天圆地方"是中国古代的一种哲学思想。天与圆象征运动，地与方象征静止，两者的结合则是阴阳平衡、动静互补。"天圆地方"的思想常常表现在中国古代的建筑设计上，例如北京的天坛与地坛。

读后思考

1. 为什么可以说金沙文明是古蜀文明的后续？

2. 为什么在古代中国，人们会有"天圆地方"的观念？

交流讨论

在你的文化中，人们对时间有哪些比喻？

亲身体验

请在成都城市景观中或在网上寻找"太阳神鸟"的图案,并拍照分享。如下图所示:

(2) Romantic Jinsha

Surprisingly, the flourishing Sanxingdui Culture underwent a significant change around 3,200 years ago, and the city was abruptly abandoned. From the unearthed relics, some pottery artifacts with distinctive features of the Sanxingdui Culture disappeared, while other previously unseen items, such as "turtle-shell divination"[1], suddenly emerged. Later on, the Sanxingdui Culture seemed to vanish. But why did it vanish at all? Was it due to strong enemies from outside world or social changes within itself? Even nowadays, historians have not been

---
[1] The ancients used tortoise shells to predict the future.

able to provide unambiguous answers.

Although historians have not solved the mystery why the Sanxingdui Culture vanished, they do find a successive culture—Jinsha Culture.

The Jinsha Culture Site is located in present-day Qingyang District of Chengdu. The Jinsha Site Museum has been built on this site. The museum boasts distinctive building styles, with a sloping design symbolizing the gradual rise of the Jinsha Culture. In the circular Relic Hall, people can see ancient remains; while in the square Exhibition Hall, the unearthed artifacts are displayed. The circular and the square shapes of these two buildings symbolize the ancient Chinese concept of "orbicular sky and rectangular earth". The two buildings now have become the landmarks of Chengdu.

Many artifacts in Jinsha Site Museum are very similar to those in the Sanxingdui Museum, such as golden masks and kneeling stone figurines. However, interestingly, these artifacts are much smaller than their counterparts in the Sanxingdui Museum. According to some historians' analysis, the social productivity of the Jinsha Culture may have been much lower than that of the Sanxingdui Culture, so it was rather difficult to duplicate large-scale objects like the bronze trees and figures.

At the center is the grand treasure of the Jinsha Site Museum, the most precious piece of cultural relics. That is, the "Sun and Immortal Birds Gold Ornament". It has a diameter of 12.5 centimeters, a thickness of 0.02 centimeters, and a weight of 20 grams. The entire

design is like a piece of Chinese paper-cutting artwork with concise and smooth lines, giving a sense of liveliness. The inner pattern consists of twelve sun rays rotating clockwise, while the outer pattern depicts four birds flying counterclockwise. Some historians believe that the twelve sun rays symbolize the twelve months of a year, while the four birds symbolize the four seasons, implying the passage of time.

As the ancient Chinese put it, "Time flies like an arrow", and as a modern song goes, "My youthful bird has flown away, never to return." Such romantic metaphors come to life in the vivid imagery of the Jinsha Culture.

Because Sichuan people are deeply fond of the Sun and Immortal Birds Gold Motif, it has been designated as the city logo of Chengdu and is used in various places such as on bus stop signs or city promotional posters. As a matter of fact, not merely being popular among Sichuan people, this design was also announced by the National Cultural Heritage Administration as the symbol of Chinese cultural heritage in 2005.

Notes

1. 再后来，三星堆文化似乎就消失了。

"似乎" is an adverb which means "as if", used as a synonym for "仿佛，好像". For example:

我似乎在什么地方见过他。

三天不见，似乎离别了三年。

Additionally, it also means "seem to (do), it seems that". For example:

这件事咱们似乎可以不用管。

这么贵的东西似乎不应该买。

2. 有历史学家分析说，金沙时期的社会生产力可能比三星堆时期要差得多，所以很难再造出像铜树和铜像那样大型的器物。

"分析" is a verb which means "to analyze". For example:

她分析出失败的原因后找到了解决的方法。

Extensive Reading

天圆地方 (tiān yuán dì fāng)

The idea of "天圆地方" is a philosophical thought in ancient China, which literally means "orbicular sky and rectangular earth". "天" and "圆" (meaning "sky" and "round") symbolize movement, while "地" and "方" (meaning "earth" and "square") symbolize stillness. The combination of the two represents the balance between Yin and Yang, and the interplay between movement and stillness. The idea of "天圆地方" is often manifested in ancient Chinese architectural designs, such as the Temple of Heaven and the Earth Altar in Beijing.

Questions

1. Why is the Jinsha Civilization considered as a continuation of the Ancient Shu Civilization?

2. Why did people hold the belief of "orbicular sky and rectangular earth" in ancient China?

Discussion

In your culture, what metaphors do people use for time?

Experience

Please look for the images of "Sun and Immortal Birds Gold Ornament" in Chengdu cityscape or online, and share your pictures as shown below:

（三）传奇三国（上）

三国时期是中国古代历史上很有名的一段时期。从 220 年到 280 年，中国有曹魏、蜀汉和东吴三个政权。其中蜀汉政权的主体部分就在今天的四川地区。当时蜀汉政权的第一个皇帝叫刘备，他认为自己的政权是汉朝的延续，所以把自己的政权称为"汉"。又因他的政权主要位于蜀地，所以后来的人为了区别，就把这一政权称为"蜀汉"。蜀汉政权一共存在了 43 年，这是四川历史上最具传奇性的时期之一。

当时的蜀汉地区要比今天的四川省大得多，大概包括今天的四川、云南和贵州，甚至到达了缅甸和越南北部。这个区域的管理工作主要由蜀汉的丞相诸葛亮来领导。诸葛是他的姓，亮是他的名。诸葛亮在中国人心目中是最优秀的政治家之一。大家认为正是由于他的杰出工作,三国时期的蜀汉地区才得到了快速发展。下面的三个例子可以说明当时蜀汉的繁华景象。

第一,当时蜀汉政权的管理范围包括很多少数民族地区,这些地区到现在很多仍然是少数民族居住的地方。在诸葛亮的领导下,蜀汉政权获得了各族人民的支持。汉族与少数民族人民一起开发蜀汉地区,实现了民族团结与共同发展。这也是现在四川地区民族关系和谐的历史基础之一。

第二,诸葛亮有一个很著名的管理理念是"务农殖谷,闭关息民"[1],主要目的就是大力发展农业,让人民生活富足。蜀汉政权不仅制定了一系列有利于农业发展的政策,而且维修了水利设施以保证农业生产。有了这些支持,本来就"土地肥美"的四川,农业发展不断加快,社会经济一片繁荣。

第三,有了农业作为经济的基础,蜀汉开始着手发展手工业。蜀汉地区的盐和铁资源丰富,制盐、冶铁两大行业迅速发展。同时,四川最著名的蜀锦业也在当时达到了一个高峰。为了更好地管理蜀锦的生产,诸葛亮还专门设置了官职"锦官"。后来成都的别名——"锦官城",就源自这个官名。

这些史实都能说明三国时期是四川地区发展的一大高峰。不过,中国历史发展的趋势总是以统一为主流。繁荣的蜀汉政权到了263年,因当时的皇帝刘禅投降魏国而宣告灭亡了。中国很快再次统一,这也就是后来的晋朝。由于四川人民很怀念蜀汉这一美好的时期,因此对那位投降的皇帝——刘禅的评价非常低,认

1　参见《三国志·蜀书·后主传》,载陈寿(晋):《三国志》,北京:中华书局,2009,第147页。

历史篇
History

为是他断送了欣欣向荣的蜀汉政权。现在在四川我们还能听到很多民间故事批评或嘲笑刘禅愚蠢。当然,历史事件的成因非常复杂,很难说是某一个人的功劳或过错。不过,通过这些故事,我们能感受到四川人对蜀汉这段历史的怀念。

语言点例释

1. 当时的蜀汉地区要比今天的四川省大得多,大概包括今天的四川、云南和贵州,甚至到达了缅甸和越南北部。

这句话的大意是"蜀汉地区甚至包括缅甸和越南北部"。其中,"……,甚至……"用在并列成分的最后一项前,表示强调,强调"甚至"后面突出的事例(有更进一层的意思),例如"20世纪90年代,中国的东部、中部,甚至西部群众的生活都有了很大的提高"。

2. 有了这些支持,本来就"土地肥美"的四川,农业发展不断加快,社会经济一片繁荣。

这句话的大意是"有了支持,四川一片繁荣"。其中,"繁荣"是形容词,意思是"(经济或事业)向好的方向发展",例如"成都是一个繁荣的城市"。"繁荣"也可以是一个动词,意思是"使(经济或事业)向好的方向发展",例如"繁荣经济,繁荣文化事业"。

延伸阅读

诸葛亮

诸葛亮字孔明,号卧龙,生活的年代是181—234年,出生在今天的山东省。他不仅是三国时期的蜀汉丞相,也是杰出的政治家、军事家、文学家、书法家、发明家。在中国人看来,他是智慧的象征。

刘禅

刘禅是蜀汉怀帝,又称后主,小名阿斗,生活的年代是207—271年,出生在今河北省。他是三国时期蜀汉的最后一位皇帝。

读后思考

1. 你知道哪些三国时期的历史故事?
2. 为什么说"三国时期是四川地区发展的一大高峰"?

第二眼看四川：
向世界讲述四川故事
Second Glance at Sichuan: Telling Sichuan Stories to the World

交流讨论

请采访一位中国朋友，请他/她谈一谈自己对诸葛亮或者刘禅的印象。

姓名	印象关键词	历史故事

(3) Legendary Three Kingdoms Period (Part I)

The Three Kingdoms Period is one of the most famous eras in the Chinese history. From 220 to 280, China was divided into three separate regimes: Cao Wei, Shu Han, and Eastern Wu. The Shu Han regime was mainly located in today's Sichuan. Liu Bei, the founder of the Shu Han regime, named his regime "Han" because he believed that his political power was a continuation of the Han Dynasty. And since his regime was primarily based in the Shu region, people later differentiated it by calling it "Shu Han". The Shu Han regime lasted for 43 years, remaining one of the most legendary Periods in Sichuan's history.

At that time, the Shu Han area was much larger than today's Sichuan province, which probably included present-day Sichuan, Yunnan, Guizhou provinces, and even the northern parts of Myanmar and Vietnam. Zhuge Liang, serving as the chancellor of Shu Han regime, was put in charge of governing such a vast territory. Zhuge is his surname, and Liang last name. Zhuge Liang is recognized as the most accomplished state governors in the eyes of the Chinese people. People believed that it is because of his outstanding work that Shu Han regime

could develop rapidly during the Three Kingdoms Period. Here are three examples to prove the prosperity of Shu Han during that time.

Firstly, the regime back on already covered many settlement areas of minorities, among which many are still predominantly inhabited by ethnic groups today. Under the leadership of Zhuge Liang, the Shu Han regime won the support of people from various ethnic groups. The Han people and minority ethnic people worked together to develop this region, achieving national unity and shared development. This has also become one of the historical foundations for the harmonious ethnic relations in Sichuan today.

Secondly, Zhuge Liang is famous for his administrative philosophy called "promoting agriculture, developing economy, and pacifying the people", devoting to vigorously developing agriculture and ensuring the people's livelihood. Leaders of the Shu Han regime not only issued a series of policies favorable for agricultural development but also refurbished water conservancy facilities to ensure agricultural production. With these measures, Sichuan, already known for its fertile and beautiful land, experienced accelerated agricultural development, leading to a prosperous socio-economic landscape.

Thirdly, with agriculture as the foundation of economy, the Shu Han regime began to focus on developing handicraft industries. Moreover, this region had abundant resources of salt and iron, leading to the rapid growth of salt-making and iron-smelting industries. In addition, the renowned Shu brocade ["蜀锦 (shǔjǐn)" in Chinese] in Sichuan reached its peak during that time. Zhuge Liang established a

specialized official position entitled "锦官 (Jǐnguān)" to manage the production of Shu brocade. Another name for Chengdu, "Jinguan City" ["锦官城 (Jǐnguānchéng)" in Chinese], originated from this official title.

All the historical facts above can demonstrate that the Three Kingdoms Period was a major development peak in Sichuan's history. However, the trend of Chinese historical development has always been focused on unity. The prosperous Shu Han came to an end in 263 when Emperor Liu Shan surrendered to the Wei regime. Later, China entered the Jin Dynasty. As Sichuan people cherished their time during the Shu Han regime, they disdained Liu Shan who was blamed for bringing about the downfall of the flourishing Shu Han. Even now Liu Shan is ridiculed and mocked in some local folk stories for his foolishness. Nonetheless, the causes of historical events are far more complicated, and it is difficult to attribute them solely to the actions or faults of one person. However, through these stories, one can certainly get a glimpse of Sichuan people's nostalgia for the Shu Han.

历史篇 History

❧ Notes ❧

1. 当时的蜀汉地区要比今天的四川省大得多, 大概包括今天的四川、云南和贵州, 甚至缅甸和越南北部。

　　This sentence basically means "蜀汉地区甚至包括缅甸和越南北部". Here, "……, 甚至……" is used before the last coordinate item to emphasize the case that stands out after "甚至". For example:

　　20世纪90年代, 中国的东部、中部甚至西部群众的生活都有了很大的提高。

2. 有了这些支持, 本来就"土地肥美"的四川, 农业发展不断加快, 社会经济一片繁荣。

　　This sentence basically means "有了支持, 四川一片繁荣". Here, "繁荣" is an adjective which means "prosperous". For example:

　　成都是一个繁荣的城市。

　　"繁荣" can also be a verb that means "to prosper". For example:

　　繁荣经济, 繁荣文化事业。

❧ Extensive Reading ❧

Zhuge Liang

Zhuge Liang (181–234), also known as Kongming or Wolong, was born in today's Shandong province. He was not only the chancellor of Shu Han during the Three Kingdoms Period but also an outstanding statesman, military strategist, litterateur, calligrapher and inventor. To the Chinese people, he is a symbol of wisdom.

Liu Shan

Liu Shan (207–271), Emperor Huai of Shu Han, also known as the Houzhu or Adou (his infant name), was born in today's Hebei province. He was the last emperor of Shu Han during the Three Kingdoms Period.

❧ Questions ❧

1. Do you know any historical story about the Three Kingdoms Period?

2. Why is it said that the Three Kingdoms Period was a major development peak in Sichuan's history?

第二眼看四川：向世界讲述四川故事
Second Glance at Sichuan: Telling Sichuan Stories to the World

Discussion

Please interview a Chinese friend about his/her impressions of Zhuge Liang or Liu Shan.

Name	Key Words of Impression	Historical Stories

（四）传奇三国（下）

三国时期的历史之所以特别有名，一个很重要的原因是小说《三国演义》的流行。《三国演义》是中国古代"四大名著"之一。这部小说讲述了三国历史上一个个激动人心的传奇故事。这个故事以蜀汉政权为正统，也就是说蜀汉一方是正面人物，因此这些人物能最多地得到人们的同情。这使得很多人来到成都一定会去武侯祠参观。武侯祠这个地方就是祭祀蜀汉英雄人物的著名祠堂。

参观之前，我们可以先了解一下这些蜀汉人物的故事。

第一个要介绍的当然是蜀汉的丞相诸葛亮。他在中国古代历史上是智慧的代表。现在有一种说法叫作"斜杠青年"，英文是"Slash"，是指一群拥有多重职业和能力的人。诸葛亮就是这样的"斜杠青年"，因为他是杰出的政治家、军事家、外交家、文学家、书法家、发明家。厉害吧？不过他最让中国人怀念的，还是作为一名政治家，他一直把老百姓的生活放在很重要的位置上，并且此为基础来制定政策。

著名的武侯祠就是纪念诸葛亮的祠堂。不过你到了门口，却会看到牌子上写着"汉昭烈祠"。你并没有走错或是看错，其实

这个地方的本名就是"汉昭烈祠",是祭祀蜀汉皇帝刘备的祠堂。但是因为老百姓太尊敬和喜爱诸葛亮,所以慢慢地,这个地方就只剩下一个名字——武侯祠。可见,诸葛亮在四川人心目中地位多么重要。

武侯祠大门

第二就必须说到"刘关张三结义"了。"刘"指刘备,是大哥;"关"指关羽,是二弟;"张"指张飞,是三弟。你可能会问,这三兄弟怎么都不是一个姓呢?那是因为他们是结拜兄弟。在中国,特别好的朋友往往愿意结拜为兄弟或者姐妹,意思是像家人一样亲密。这三个兄弟互相支持,共同努力,建立了蜀汉政权,也为蜀汉的发展做出了很大的贡献。这三人忠义的美好品质和他们之间真诚、深切的友谊受到后人的崇拜。

武侯祠里面专门设有"三义庙"以纪念他们。"三"当然指三位英雄,"义"则是指义气。"刘关张"在中国文化中已经成为义气的代名词。

第三要说一个武侯祠里面看不到的人物——刘禅。按理说,刘禅是刘备的儿子,是蜀汉的第二个皇帝,应该是会出现在祠堂

第二眼看四川：
向世界讲述四川故事
Second Glance at Sichuan: Telling Sichuan Stories to the World

里的。但是由于后人不满他带领蜀汉走向灭亡，所以干脆取消了他的位置。直到今天，四川人大都不称呼他刘禅，而是称他"阿斗"——这是刘禅的小名。在中国人看来，如果不是家人，称呼一个人的小名就是看不起他的意思。汉语中还有一句俗话是"扶不起的阿斗"，就是指不论别人怎么样帮助都没有进步的人。

除此之外，蜀汉最重要的28名官员也都有各自的塑像，被列在武侯祠的"文武廊"。喜欢三国文化的朋友去了，都会仔细阅读各塑像旁边的名片，因为这里的每个人物都是一段传奇。

语言点例释

1. 但是因为老百姓太尊敬和喜爱诸葛亮，所以慢慢地，这个地方就只剩下一个名字——武侯祠。

"尊敬"是动词，意思是"严肃、礼貌地对待（地位或品德崇高的人）"，例如"尊敬老师，受人尊敬"。"尊敬"还可以作形容词，意思是"可尊敬的"，例如"尊敬的女士们，先生们"。需要注意的是，"尊敬"一般是指晚辈对长辈的敬重或下级对上级的崇拜，例如"尊敬老人，尊敬的校长"。

2. 直到今天，四川人大都不称呼他刘禅，而是称他"阿斗"。

"大都"是一个范围副词，在句子中作状语，表示某一范围内的人或物的大部分都具有某种倾向、性质、状况，例如"中国的南方人大都喜欢吃大米"；"参加排球比赛的大都是女生"。

延伸阅读

锦里

武侯祠的旁边有一条热闹非凡的小街，叫作"锦里"。传说这条街在三国时期就已经闻名全国。现在这条街是成都最有名的旅游地标之一，是人们体验三国文化、品尝四川小吃的好地方。

读后思考

1. 武侯祠中为什么没有蜀汉皇帝——刘禅的位置？

2. 在三国时期的蜀汉人物中，你对哪个人物最感兴趣？为什么？

交流讨论

你怎么理解中国人口中的"义气"？在你的文化中有相似的说法吗？有哪些人物是义气的代表？

亲身体验

请你在武侯祠中分别找到诸葛亮、刘备、关羽和张飞的塑像，并拍照分享。

(4) Legendary Three Kingdoms Period (Part II)

One of the most important reasons why the Three Kingdoms Period is particularly famous is the popularity of the novel *Romance of the Three Kingdoms*, which is regarded as one of the Four Great Classical Novels of ancient Chinese literature. In this novel, the history of the Three Kingdoms Period is told in a series of exciting legendary tales. The Shu Han regime is portrayed as the rightful and heroic side, which evokes sympathy from readers. This has led many people to visit Wuhou Shrine (Temple of Marquis Wu) in Chengdu, which is a famous memorial temple for worshiping heroes of Shu Han.

Check out some of the most well-known figures and stories of Shu Han before paying a visit!

The first hero that one must know is of course, Zhuge Liang, the grand chancellor of Shu Han, who is the embodiment of wisdom in ancient Chinese history. In recent days, a new concept that emerged

Second Glance at Sichuan: Telling Sichuan Stories to the World

on the Internet—"Slash", is used to describe individuals with multiple identities, careers and talents. Zhuge Liang was indeed a Slash, who was an outstanding statesman, strategist, diplomat, writer, calligrapher, inventor. Impressive, isn't it? However, what truly makes Chinese people nostalgic about him is his role as a state governor who always prioritized the well-being of the common people and developed policies based on that principle.

The famous Wuhou Shrine is indeed a temple dedicated to the memory of Zhuge Liang. However, when getting to the entrance, one will see a plaque that reads "Zhaolie Temple of Han". This, not a mistake, was indeed the original name of this place, a memorial temple in honor of Emperor Liu Bei. However, due to the much deeper respect and affection the common people have for Zhuge Liang, gradually, this place has come to be known simply as "Wuhou Shrine". It can be seen that how important Zhuge Liang is in the minds of Sichuan people.

The second story that must be mentioned is the "Oath of the Peach Garden", which bound three brothers: Liu, Guan, and Zhang, respectively referring to Liu Bei, the eldest brother, Guan Yu, the second, and the youngest Zhang Fei. People may wonder why these three brothers have different surnames. That is because they were sworn brothers. In China, really good friends are willing to become sworn brothers or sisters, as close as family members. The three brothers supported each other and worked together, establishing the Shu Han regime and making great contributions to the development of it. Later, their virtuous qualities of loyalty and righteousness, as well as their

sincere and profound friendship, became admired by future generations.

In the Wuhou Shrine, there is a special hall called "Sanyi Temple" built in commemoration of them. The word "san" means "three", naturally referring to the three heroes, and "yi" refers to means loyalty. Therefore, "Liu-Guan-Zhang" has become synonymous with loyalty and righteousness in Chinese culture.

The third is Liu Shan, a historical figure who cannot be found in Wuhou Shrine. People outside Sichuan may assume that Liu Shan, the son of Liu Bei and the second emperor of Shu Han, should have his place in the memorial temple. However, due to the dislike and blame he received for leading Shu Han to its downfall, unsurprisingly, people did not make room for him. To this day, most people in Sichuan call him by his infant name "Adou" ["阿斗 (Ādǒu)" in Chinese], not Liu Shan. In China, being called one's infant name by a non-family member can be seen as a sign of disrespect. Moreover, there is also a popular Chinese saying "扶不起的阿斗 (fúbùqǐ de Ādǒu)", which is used to describe incapable people who would not achieve anything even with significant assistance.

In addition, the statues of the 28 most important officials of Shu Han are also displayed in the Civil and Military Officer Gallery of the Wuhou Shrine. People who appreciate the culture of the Three Kingdoms Period should carefully read every name tag beside each statue, because each one boasts a legendary tale.

第二眼看四川：向世界讲述四川故事
Second Glance at Sichuan: Telling Sichuan Stories to the World

 Notes

1. 但是因为老百姓太崇拜和尊敬诸葛亮，所以慢慢地，这个地方就只剩下一个名字——武侯祠。

"尊敬" is a verb which means "to respect". For example:

尊敬老师 / 受人尊敬。

"尊敬" can also be an adjective which means "respectable". For example:

尊敬的女士们、先生们。

It is important to note that "尊敬" generally refers to the respect of the younger generations to the older generations or the subordinates to the superiors. For example:

尊敬老人 / 尊敬的校长。

2. 直到今天，四川人大都不称呼他刘禅，而是称他"阿斗"。

"大都" is an adverb emphasizing degree which means "for the most part; mostly", and it can be used as a modifier of a sentence. For example:

中国的南方人大都喜欢吃大米。

参加排球比赛的大都是女生。

 Extensive Reading

Jinli Street

Next to the Wuhou Shrine is a very bustling and lively street called "Jinli". Legend has it that this street was already nationally famous during the Three Kingdoms Period. Now this street is one of the most renowned tourist landmarks in Chengdu, which is a good place for people to experience the culture of the Three Kingdoms Period and indulge in delicious Sichuan cuisine.

Questions

1. Why is there no place for Liu Shan, the second emperor of the Shu Han regime, in Wuhou Shrine?

2. Which figure from Shu Han during the Three Kingdoms Period interests you most? Why?

History

Discussion

How to understand the term "义气 (yìqi)" in Chinese culture? Is there any similar concept in your culture? Which figures can be described by "义气" in your culture?

Experience

Please look for the statues of Zhuge Liang, Liu Bei, Guan Yu, and Zhang Fei in the Wuhou Shrine or on its official website, and share your photos of them.

五、古迹篇

往事在风中飘散,唯有古迹留在我们身边。本篇为你讲述四川历史的"证物"。

5. Historical Sites

The past may have gone with the wind, but the historical sites stand beside us indeed. This chapter represents the "evidence" of Sichuan's history.

第二眼看四川：向世界讲述四川故事
Second Glance at Sichuan: Telling Sichuan Stories to the World

（一）"天府之国"的守卫——都江堰

我们都知道万里长城是中国的一大象征。很多人认为，长城代表了中国人的聪明才智和坚强毅力。没错，在2000多年前的秦朝，人们能够修建像长城这么宏大的工程，非常值得敬佩。但是也有人认为，其实在长城之前，有一个同样宏大的工程已经建成。而且更可贵的是，这一工程至今仍在发挥作用，守护着人们的日常生活。从某种意义上讲，这个工程更能够体现中国人的智慧和才华，是中国文化的杰出代表。这就是位于四川省成都市的都江堰。

都江堰

都江堰的"都江"指的就是成都的江，"堰"指的是围住水的坝。都江堰位于成都平原西部的岷江上，修建于约公元前256年—前251年。岷江是长江上游水量最大的一条支流，由无数条来自高山之间的河流汇集而成，到了雨季，岷江的水就会迅速地涨起来。对于成都平原来说，岷江的位置很高，一旦涨水，整个平原就会变成大海。可想而知，岷江的水患长期影响着四川的农业发展和人民的生活。

都江堰正位于岷江进入成都平原的入口处。这一工程的整体规划是将岷江水流分成两条，只将其中一条引入成都平原。这样成都既可以利用岷江水发展农业，又可以避免水患之灾。具体来说，都江堰可以分成三大部分：宝瓶口、分水鱼嘴和飞沙堰。下面我们具体说说这三大部分有什么功能。

第一步修建的是宝瓶口。准确地说，宝瓶口是炸出来的。当时人们用火烧石头，把堵住岷江的一座山炸出一个口子。因为这个口子看起来像一个瓶子，所以叫宝瓶口。这样岷江水就多了一条通路，不会一下雨就上涨得那么快，而且江水还能流向更广大的地方，支持农业生产。

第二步修建的是分水鱼嘴。这个部分将岷江水分为两条支流，确保有一部分水流入宝瓶口。

第三步修建的是飞沙堰。为了进一步控制进入宝瓶口的水量，人们又修建了飞沙堰，如果进入宝瓶口的水太多，就会通过飞沙堰的调节进入另一条支流排出。

除此之外，人们还在水中放了三座石人像，它们就像三把尺子，用来观测流入成都平原的水量，以便人们提前做好准备。正是有了都江堰，成都才成为"天府之国"。两千多年来，都江堰一直守护着四川的土地和人民。

还记得这一大型水利工程是谁主持修建的吗？没错！就是秦国的官员李冰。后来人们把都江堰附近的一座庙改建为"二王庙"，以此纪念李冰父子。另外，在都江堰，游客还能看到一座美丽的索桥，叫作"安澜桥"。整座桥以石头做底座，以竹索为栏杆，非常具有四川西部的特色。

第二眼看四川：向世界讲述四川故事
Second Glance at Sichuan: Telling Sichuan Stories to the World

安澜桥

从都江堰，我们可以看到人与自然的和谐相处：人们保护自然，利用自然；而自然支持人们的生产生活。都江堰充分显示了中国人的勇气和智慧，在2000年被联合国列入"世界遗产名录"。

语言点例释

1. 对于成都平原来说，岷江的位置很高，一旦涨水，整个平原就会变成大海。

　　这句话的大意是"岷江一旦涨水，成都平原就会变成大海"。其中，"一旦……，就……"表示假设，前一个分句提出一个假设的情况，后一个分句说明由假设情况产生的结果或推论，例如"一旦考试不及格，我就要延期毕业了"。

2. 为了进一步控制进入宝瓶口的水量，人们又修建了飞沙堰，如果进入宝瓶口的水太多，就会通过飞沙堰的调节进入另一条支流排出。

　　这句话的大意是"飞沙堰控制了进入宝瓶口的水量"。其中，"控制"是一个动词，意思是"掌握事物的变化，使其在一定的范围内"，例如"这次活动需要控制人数，不能超过一百人"。

读后思考

1. 都江堰的总体治水思路是什么？整个工程分为哪三个部分？

古迹篇
Historical Sites

2. 为什么说"从都江堰,我们可以看到人与自然的和谐相处"?

❀ 交流讨论 ❀

除了都江堰,你还知道四川有哪些名胜古迹被列入"世界遗产名录"?

(1) Dujiangyan: Guardian of the "Land of Abundance"

It is known to all that the Great Wall is a significant symbol of China, which is considered by many people as a representative of the intelligence and perseverance of the Chinese people. It is indeed admirable that over 2,000 years ago, during the Qin Dynasty, such a grand project like the Great Wall was constructed. But many people believe that another equally magnificent project had been completed even earlier than the Great Wall. What is more valuable is that this project still has practical functions today, protecting people's daily lives. In a sense, this project better embodies the wisdom and talent of the Chinese people and stands as an outstanding representative of Chinese culture. This is Dujiangyan Irrigation System in Chengdu, Sichuan province.

"Dujiang" in Dujiangyan refers to the rivers in Chengdu, while "yan" means a dam to stop the water from flowing. Located on the Minjiang River on the west of the Chengdu Plain, Dujiangyan was built between 256 BC and 251 BC. The Minjiang River is the largest tributary of the upper reaches of the Yangtze River, formed by numerous

rivers flowing from the mountains. Therefore, during Periods of heavy rainfall, the water level of the Minjiang River rises rapidly. Given the high elevation of the Minjiang River in relation to the Chengdu Plain, once it flooded, the entire plain would be submerged. Recurring floods of the Minjiang River have long affected the agricultural development and people's lives in Sichuan.

Dujiangyan is located at the entrance of the Minjiang River into the Chengdu Plain. The overall plan of this project is to divert the Minjiang River into two flows, allowing only one of them to enter the Chengdu Plain. In this way, Chengdu can not only utilize the water of the Minjiang River for agricultural development, but also avoid floods. To be more specific, Dujiangyan is divided into three major parts: Bottle-Neck Channel, Fish-Mouth Levee, and Feishayan Weir. The functions of these three parts in details are as below.

The first part was the Bottle-Neck Channel which was formed by rock blasting. People at that time used fire to burn stones to blow up a hole in the mountain that blocked the Minjiang River. The hole resembled a bottle, so it was called the Bottle-Neck Channel. As thus, the Minjiang River had an additional channel, preventing rapid rises in water level during rainfall and diverting the river flow into wider areas to support agricultural production.

The second part completed was the Fish-Mouth Levee, which divided the Minjiang River into two streams, ensuring that some of the water would enter the Bottle-Neck Channel.

The third part was the Feishayan Weir, or the Flying Sand Weir,

built to further control the amount of water entering the Bottle-Neck Channel. In this way, the excessive river water would be regulated and diverted to another channel.

What's more, people also placed three stone statues in the water, resembling three gauges, to observe the water levels flowing into the Chengdu Plain in order to make preparations in advance. It was with the construction of Dujiangyan that Chengdu has become the "Land of Abundance". For more than two thousand years, Dujiangyan has been protecting Sichuan and its people. As mentioned in the earlier chapters, Li Bing, an official of Qin state was the one who directed the construction of this large-scale project. Later, a temple near Dujiangyan was converted into "Two Kings Temple" to commemorate Li Bing and his son. Additionally, in Dujiangyan city, visitors can also find a beautiful suspension bridge called Anlan Suspension Bridge. It has a stone base and bamboo ropes as its railings, which is full of distinctive characteristics of Western Sichuan.

From Dujiangyan, the harmony between humans and nature can be witnessed: people protect nature and make use of nature, while nature supports people's production and lives. Dujiangyan Irrigation System shows the courage and wisdom of the Chinese people. It was listed as a World Heritage List by UNESCO in 2000.

第二眼看四川：
向世界讲述四川故事
Second Glance at Sichuan: Telling Sichuan Stories to the World

Notes

1. 对于成都平原来说，岷江的位置很高，一旦涨水，整个平原就会变成大海。

  This sentence basically means "岷江一旦涨水，成都平原就会变成大海". Here, "一旦……，就……" indicates suppositive relation that one clause puts forward an assumption while the other one states the result or inference drawn from the assumption. For example:

  一旦考试不及格，我就要延期毕业了。

2. 为了进一步控制进入宝瓶口的水量，人们又修建了飞沙堰，如果进入宝瓶口的水太多，就会通过飞沙堰的调节进入另一条支流排出。

  This sentence basically means "飞沙堰控制了进入宝瓶口的水量". Here, "控制" is a verb which means "to control, to restrict". For example:

  这次活动需要控制人数，不能超过一百人。

Questions

1. What is the overall water-management strategy of Dujiangyan? What are the three major parts of it?

2. Why do people say "from Dujiangyan, the harmony between humans and nature can be witnessed"?

Discussion

Besides Dujiangyan, do you know which other places of interest in Sichuan that have been listed as a UNESCO "World Heritage List"?

（二）古代战场的见证——剑门关

  除了武侯祠，四川还有很多与三国文化有关的古代遗迹。剑门关就是其中很著名的一处。

  剑门关的"关"指的是中国古代在交通要道上设置的防卫地。简单地说，古代没有飞机，人们只要控制住陆地上的路就可以防止敌人进入自己的国家了。所以，人们往往会在连接两个地方的交通道路上设计一个可以驻扎军队的地方，这个地方当然要易守，要难被敌人进入。这样的地方就被称为"关"。中国有很多有名的关，比如长城上的山海关。而剑门关，我们可以理解成是古时候从北方进入四川地区的一个门，所以"剑门"也叫作"蜀门"，就是进入四川的大门。

唐朝著名诗人李白曾经写道，剑门关是"一夫当关，万夫莫开"，意思就是一个人守着门，一万个人来攻打也不能进入。当然这个说法是有点夸张，但是你到了剑门关，就会发现这说法也许有点儿道理。剑门关的关楼，给人的感觉是被塞在两排高山之间，楼的两边没有路走，山上也没有路走。所以要想进入四川就只能从门里面走。但是进入门的道路非常狭窄，大概只能并排走两三个人，所以敌人的军队根本没有办法进入。这样的地势就是剑门关得名的原因，因为两边的山就像两把宝剑一样又高又直，组成一道大门，所以就叫剑门。

剑门关主要是由三国时期的丞相诸葛亮主持修建的。这当然是出于军事上的需要：有了这样的门，四川的军队出得去，别的军队却进不来。虽然一个人守门、一万个人也进不来的说法有点夸张，但是在三国时期一场著名的战争中，3万人的四川军队的确把敌人的10万人成功挡在了门外。

除了关楼，剑门关的栈道也让人惊叹。因为这里的山都非常陡峭，无路可走，所以传说中诸葛亮就发明了栈道。他命令人们在山上打出一个个的洞，插入木头，做成栈道。你能想象吗？整条栈道都是悬空的！

栈道

  说到道路，剑门关还有一条古代的道路也很有特色，名字叫"翠云廊"。"廊"是通道的意思，那为什么叫作绿色的云廊呢？是因为这条道路两旁种着美丽的柏树。这些生长了一千多年的树又高又直，树叶就像连绵的绿色的云。走在这条路上，很少能照到阳光，有一种千年时光静止的感觉。在这里，多少人经过，多少人战死？一年又一年，树木都差不多，但是人却完全不同了。不过这些树在当时可不仅仅是为了好看，而是有很重要的功能。首先是保护道路，避免雨水破坏道路；其次是为修建栈道准备木材，免得从很远的地方运来木头。

  走过关门，经过古道，在游览了两三个小时以后，你一定饿

古迹篇
Historical Sites

了。那么不妨尝尝这里的豆腐,名叫剑门豆腐。传说,这也是三国时期的四川军队发明的。虽然不知道这个传说是不是真的,不过好吃是真的。与四川一般的豆腐相比,这里的豆腐色泽雪白,口感细腻,而且用豆腐做的菜式特别多,一定能让你大饱口福。

语言点例释

1. 他命令人们在山上打出一个个的洞,插入木头,做成栈道。

"命令"在这句话中是一个动词,意思是"上级指示下级去做某事",例如"老板命令我今晚必须完成任务"。"命令"也可以是一个名词,意思是"上级给下级的指示",例如"下达命令,执行命令"。

2. 那么不妨尝尝这里的豆腐,名叫剑门豆腐。

"不妨"是一个副词,表示没有妨碍,不会产生消极影响。需要注意的是,"不妨"多用于建议,常有尝试的意思,后面的动词多为"试试、尝一下、看一看"等,例如"据说这个药效果很好,你不妨试一试"。

拓展阅读

栈道

"栈道"是中国古代交通史上的一大发明。为了在深山峡谷中通行,人们在山壁上凿出一些孔,插上石桩或木桩,然后在上面铺上木板或石板,变成路。同时,为了防止这些木桩和木板被雨淋而腐烂,又在栈道的最高处建起亭子。

读后思考

1. 剑门关为什么能做到"一夫当关,万夫莫开"?
2. 翠云廊的树木有哪些功能?

交流讨论

你的国家有没有像"关"一样的防止外敌入侵的地方?请互相分享。

Second Glance at Sichuan: Telling Sichuan Stories to the World

(2) Jianmen Pass: Witness to Ancient Battlefield

Apart from the Wuhou Shrine, there are many ancient relics related to the culture of the Three Kingdoms Period in Sichuan, among which, Jianmen Pass is quite famous.

The word "pass" in Jianmen Pass refers to the defensive strongholds set up on the major traffic arteries in ancient times. In short, due to the lack of air transportation back then, people could only prevent their enemies from entering their country by controlling the land routes. Therefore, people tended to design a place along the routes to connect two locations where troops could be stationed. Of course, this place needed to be easily guarded but difficult for enemies to break in. Such a place is called "pass" ["关 (guān)" in Chinese], and there are many famous passes in China, such as Shanhai Pass on the Great Wall. Jianmen Pass, as a gate leading into Sichuan from the north in ancient times, is also called "Shumen" ("Shu" is short for Sichuan province), which means the gateway to Sichuan.

Li Bai, a famous poet in the Tang Dynasty, once wrote "one man guards the pass, ten thousand cannot pass", indicating that even if ten thousand people tried to attack, they couldn't enter Sichuan as long as just one person guarded the pass. This is, of course, an exaggeration, but one may find there is some truth to it when visiting Jianmen Pass. Jianmen Pass tower gives the impression of being wedged between two rows of high mountains, with no paths neither along both sides of the tower nor on the mountains, hence going through the gate was the only way to enter Sichuan. However, the entrance to the gate is far too

古迹篇
Historical Sites

narrow, allowing only three people to walk side by side, which makes it impossible for enemy troops to enter. This unique terrain is also the reason for the name of Jianmen Pass. The mountains on both sides are as high and straight as two swords, forming a gateway, thus it is called Jianmen Pass which literally means "Sword Gate".

Jianmen Pass was primarily built under the supervision of Zhuge Liang out of military necessity: with such a pass, the Sichuan army could go out, but enemy forces could not come in. Although it was somewhat exaggerating to say that "one man guards the pass, ten thousand cannot pass", during a famous war of the Three Kingdoms Period, the Sichuan army of 30,000 managed to keep an enemy force of 100,000 out.

In addition to the pass tower, the gallery roads of Jianmen Pass are also amazing. Because the mountains here are very steep and there is no way to find a pathway, it was said that Zhuge Liang invented the gallery roads. He commanded people to burrow into the cliffs and then insert wooden planks to make roads. Indeed, it is difficult to believe the entire pathway is suspended in mid-air!

When it comes to roads, there is also an ancient road with unique characteristics in Jianmen Pass, whose name is "Cuiyunlang", or "Cuiyun Corridor". "Lang" refers to the passageway, but why is it called "Cuiyunlang" (literally means "green cloud corridor")? That is because the road is lined with beautiful cypress trees that have been alive for more than a thousand years, tall and straight, with the leaves like continuous green clouds. Walking along this road, one can feel little sunlight but a sense of time standing still for a thousand years. How

第二眼看四川：
向世界讲述四川故事
Second Glance at Sichuan: Telling Sichuan Stories to the World

many people have passed through here, and how many people have fallen in warfare? Year after year, the trees remain almost the same, but the people have completely changed. However, not just for decoration, these trees had important functions at that time. Firstly, they protected the roads, preventing rainwater damage. Secondly, they prepared the necessary timber for the construction of the gallery roads, so as not to transport wood from distant locations.

After two or three hours of passing through the pass gate and walking along the ancient pathway, one must be hungry. It is strongly suggested to try the tofu here, which is known as Jianmen Tofu. Legend has it that it was invented by the Sichuan army during the Three Kingdoms Period, which is not verifiable though. The tofu is really tasty. Compared with the regular tofu in Sichuan, Jianmen Tofu is known for its snow-white color and delicate texture. And cooked with numerous recipes, it will certainly satisfy everyone's taste buds.

Notes

1. 他命令人们在山上打出一个个的洞，插入木头，做成栈道。
   "命令" is a verb which means "to order". For example:
   老板命令我今晚必须完成任务。
   "命令" can also be a noun that means "order". For example:
   下达命令 / 执行命令

2. 那么不妨尝尝这里的豆腐，名叫剑门豆腐。
   "不妨" is an adverb used to mean "there is no harm in, might as well". It is important to note that "不妨" is often used for advice, followed by the verbs such as "试试、尝一下、看一看". For example:
   据说这个药效果很好，你不妨试一试。

古迹篇
Historical Sites

Extensive Reading

Gallery Road

Gallery road, also known as plank road or cliff road, is a great invention in ancient Chinese transportation history. In order to pass through deep mountains and valleys, people carved holes and inserted stone or wooden stakes. And then they placed wooden or stone planks on top, creating a pathway. Additionally, in order to prevent the stakes and planks from rotting due to rainwater, pavilions were built at the highest point of the gallery road.

Questions

1. Why was Jianmen Pass regarded as "one man guards the pass, ten thousand cannot pass"?

2. What are the functions of the trees in Cuiyun Corridor?

Discussion

Does your country have any place similar to the "pass" that serves as defense against foreign invasions? Please share with each other.

（三）诗意生活之感动——杜甫草堂

杜甫草堂和武侯祠可能是成都市区内最有名的两个景点了。前面我们已经说了武侯祠，这里我们来聊一聊杜甫草堂。

首先看名字，你听说过杜甫这位诗人吗？这是一位和李白齐名的唐代诗人。中国人常说，年轻人也许更喜欢李白，但是过了中年，经历过很多事情之后，就会更爱杜甫。杜甫比李白小十几岁，生活在唐朝社会由盛转衰的时期。在这一时期，他看到了战争的残酷和普通人生活的苦难，于是写下了很多关注普通人生活情况的诗。这些诗不仅非常有文采，而且记录下了很多历史的实际情况,所以人们把杜甫称为"诗圣",即写诗的圣人,把他的诗称为"诗史",意思是以诗写成的历史。

因为生活的年代充满了战争,所以杜甫一生都很辛苦,直到来到成都。在朋友的帮助下,他和家人在美丽的浣花溪旁修建了一间茅草房子,也就是今天我们看到的"草堂"。

杜甫草堂

当然,我们今天看到的"草堂"是后来的人按照当时的一些记录重新修建的。你在生活中可能从来没住过茅草房吧?是啊,现在哪儿还有用草做成的房子呢?不过想象一下,我们就能知道草房子一定是很简陋的,特别是刮风下雨的时候,要不然是屋顶上的草被风带走,要不然就是外边下大雨、里边下小雨。这些情况杜甫在自己的诗里都生动地写过。但是他写的时候并不是很愁苦的感觉,相反是有点开玩笑的、很乐观的态度。其实,这段在成都的时光,可以说是杜甫和家人们最顺利最开心的时光了。他们在这里不过居住了4年,但是杜甫却在此写了240首诗。难怪曾经有一位诗人说,人们提到杜甫诗时,可以忽略他出生和去世

古迹篇
Historical Sites

的地方，但是总不会忘了草堂。[1]

　　因此，很多人，特别是喜欢文学的人，到了成都就一定要去杜甫草堂看一看。你说你并不了解杜甫的诗？没关系，即使是不了解的游客也能在这里获得诗意的感动。夏天我们能够看到草堂的荷花盛开，下面有小鱼游来游去；冬天又有梅花展览，甚至比春天更加美丽。这些场景都在杜甫的诗中提到过，那可是1000多年前的美景啊！是不是有一种穿越回唐朝的感觉？

　　除了景色，草堂的工作人员还复原了很多唐朝的有诗意的活动。例如每年都会举行的"草堂听琴"，会邀请古琴的演奏家来表演。美妙的琴声还原了草堂的安宁和美好。再如，每年的农历正月初七会举行"草堂人日"。"人日"是正月初七的另一种说法。这一活动的来源是杜甫和好朋友在"人日"这一天互相写诗来表达想念之情。后来人们为了纪念他们之间的深切感情，都在这一天来到杜甫草堂，读诗、赏花，享受成都的诗意生活。

　　另外值得一提的是，我们还能在杜甫草堂看到一处唐代普通民居的遗址，从中能够看到当年普通老百姓的房子的大概建筑情况和使用过的一些东西。这家人和今天的我们一样，都拥有自己真实而美好的生活，或许这也就是四川文化常常带给大家的感动吧。

语言点例释

1. 夏天我们能够看到草堂的荷花盛开，下面有小鱼游来游去；冬天又有梅花展览，甚至比春天更加美丽。
　　"A来A去"是一个固定格式，表示动作的多次重复，例如"想来想去，飞来飞去，讨论来讨论去"。
2. 例如每年都会举行的"草堂听琴"，会邀请古琴的演奏家来表演。
　　"邀请"是一个动词，意思是"有礼貌地请人参加某一活动"，例如"他邀请全班同学参加他的生日会"。

1　冯至：《杜甫传》，北京：百花文艺出版社，2007年，第2页。

第二眼看  ：
向世界讲述四川故事
Second Glance at Sichuan: Telling Sichuan Stories to the World

读后思考

1. 谈一谈你所了解的杜甫。

2. 在你看来，什么样的生活能称得上是"诗意"呢？

亲身体验

杜甫草堂里有很多对联，请你去游玩时尝试读一读，也可以拍照以后和老师、同学分享。

你最喜欢的对联
上联：
下联：
对联的意思：
你为什么喜欢：

(3) Du Fu Thatched Cottage: Reminder of a Poetic Life

Du Fu Thatched Cottage and the Wuhou Shrine are probably two of the most famous attractions in Chengdu. This section gives a brief introduction to Du Fu Thatched Cottage.

Have you ever heard of the poet Du Fu? He is a renowned poet in the Tang Dynasty, who is on par with Li Bai in terms of fame. Chinese people often say that young people may like Li Bai more, but after having been experiencing more in midlife, they tend to develop a greater appreciation for Du Fu. Du Fu was over ten years younger than Li Bai, so he lived in the Period of Tang society changing from prosperity to decadence. During this Period, he witnessed the cruelty of war and people's suffering of life, which led him to write many poems focusing on the lives of ordinary people. These poems were not only written with great talent, but also recorded many historical facts. Therefore, Du Fu is revered as the "Poet Sage", and his poems are regarded as "Poetic History", capturing the essence of history through poetry.

Because of living in such turbulent times, Du Fu's life was very hard till he came to Chengdu. With the help of his friends, he and his family built a thatched cottage by the beautiful Huanhuaxi Creek, which is what we see today as the "Thatched Cottage". Of course, the Thatched Cottage was reconstructed by later generations based on historical records. Perhaps modern people have never lived in a thatched cottage, right? Indeed, nowadays houses made of straw are hardly seen. However, one can certainly imagine that a straw house must have been very shabby and poor, especially in windy or rainy days. Either the straw on the roof would be blown away by the wind or it would rain heavily outside while trickling inside. Du Fu wrote about these situations in detail in his poems. However, instead of developing a sense of deep sorrow, he expressed his feelings in a slightly humorous and optimistic way. In fact, the period Du Fu spent in Chengdu could be the most successful as well as the happiest time for him and his family. They lived there for only four years, during which Du Fu wrote 240 poems. It's no wonder that a poet once said that when people mention Du Fu's poetry, they may overlook his birthplace and place of death, but they will always remember the Thatched Cottage.

This is why many people, especially those literature lovers, make it a point to visit Du Fu Thatched Cottage in Chengdu. Even visitors who are not familiar with Du Fu's poetry can still feel his poetic passion here. In summer, one can see the lotus flowers in full bloom, with little fish swimming beneath them. In winter, the plum blossoms become even more beautiful than in spring. All these lovely scenes have been mentioned in Du Fu's poems over 1,000 years ago! Doesn't it give one a feeling of traveling back to the Tang Dynasty?

Besides the sceneries, the staff at the Thatched Cottage also organize many poetic activities to recreate the atmosphere of the Tang Dynasty. For example, there is an annual music event called "草堂听琴 (cǎo táng tīng qín)" in Chinese, inviting musicians to play Guqin (or Chinese zither). The wonderful melodies restore the tranquility and beauty of the cottage. In addition, every seventh day of the first lunar month is celebrated as the "People's Day at the Thatched Cottage", which originated from the story that Du Fu and his good friend wrote poems on that day to express their longing for each other. Later, in order to commemorate their deep friendship, people gather at Du Fu Thatched Cottage on this day, reading poems, appreciating flowers as well as enjoying the poetic life of Chengdu.

Moreover, it is worth mentioning that one can also appreciate the remains of an ordinary residential house from the Tang Dynasty here, where one can get a glimpse of the typical architectural features of ordinary residential houses and some items used by ordinary people back then. This family, just like us, had their own real and beautiful lives, which is the touching essence that Sichuan culture often brings to everyone.

古迹篇
Historical Sites

> **Notes**
>
> 1. 夏天我们能够看到草堂的荷花盛开，下面有小鱼游来游去；冬天又有梅花展览，甚至比春天更加美丽。
>
> "A 来 A 去" is a fixed phrase which indicates the repetition of an action. For example:
>
> 想来想去 / 飞来飞去 / 讨论来讨论去。
>
> 2. 例如每年都会举行的"草堂听琴"，会邀请古琴的演奏家来表演。
>
> "邀请" is a verb which means "to invite". For example:
>
> 他邀请全班同学参加他的生日会。

Questions

1. Please talk about what you know about Du Fu.

2. In your opinion, what kind of life is poetic?

Experience

There are many couplets at Du Fu Thatched Cottage. Please read them carefully and take photos during your visit, and then share them with others.

Your favorite couplet
The first line of the couplet:
The second line of the couplet:
Meaning:
The reason(s) why you like it:

（四）道教文化的代表——青羊宫

道教是中国最重要的宗教之一，而且是从一开始就起源于中国的一种宗教。但是你知道道教具体起源于中国哪个地方吗？猜到了吗？是的，就是东汉时从四川地区开始，然后传到中国其他

第二眼看四川：
向世界讲述四川故事
Second Glance at Sichuan: Telling Sichuan Stories to the World

地方。因此，道教与四川文化之间的关系特别紧密。在四川有很多道观，也就是道教的庙宇，其中最著名的就是青羊宫了。

我们先来看看青羊宫这个名字。为什么叫"青羊"呢？在传说中，当年有一个人听老子讲《道德经》，讲到一半，老子有事要走，于是让这个人过一段时间来成都青羊肆找自己。后来，老子果然就在青羊肆讲完了《道德经》。青羊肆的肆，意思是市场，也就是说，这是一个买卖一种青黑色羊的市场。后来因为道教尊老子为道教的创立者，《道德经》为道教的最高经典之一，所以人们就根据这个故事在青羊肆这个地方建立了一座道观，叫作青羊观。

到了唐朝，有一位皇帝路过成都，就在青羊观里住下。后来他回到首都之后，为了感谢青羊观道士的接待，送来很多钱。于是，道士们用这笔钱扩大了青羊观，并且把青羊观改名为青羊宫，显示这是皇帝住过的庙宇。因为这个原因，青羊宫成为唐朝最有影响力的道教场所之一。

青羊宫里最著名的是两只铜做的青羊雕像，分别是清朝的两位信仰道教的人捐给青羊宫的。左边的青羊是单角，右边的是双角。左边的羊特别有意思，身上有十二生肖的特征——鼠耳、牛身、虎爪、兔背、龙角、蛇尾、马嘴、羊胡、猴头、鸡眼、狗肚和猪屁股。民间传说这是一只神羊，只要摸一摸哪个部位，自己那个地方就不疼了。所以你到了青羊宫就能发现，这只羊身上已被大家摸得发亮。实际上，我们现在能摸的青羊是现代人模仿文物做成的，样子虽然一模一样，但是比文物要大得多。至于这个文物，你可以到青羊宫的展览馆里去欣赏。

古迹篇
Historical Sites

青羊宫的铜羊

每年农历二月十五日，青羊宫会举办青羊花会。根据民间传说，这一天是百花仙子的生日，人们称之为"花朝节"。同时，道教认为这一天是老子的生日，因此从唐朝开始，每年这一天青羊宫都会举办法事活动。可以说，到青羊宫赶花会是成都最有名的传统风俗之一了。到了这一天，信仰道教的人们会早早地到青羊宫纪念老子生日；不信道教的人，也会来看看各种漂亮的花，尝尝风味小吃，感受春天的到来。在古代，青羊花会从二月十五日开始持续一个月，好一场春天的盛会！到了现在，虽然盛会的时间没有那么长，但是人们参加花会的兴致却同样不减。可见，青羊宫和四川其他的宗教场所一样，和谐地把宗教与日常生活联系在了一起，信教的人和不信教的人可以顺利地沟通，一起享受美丽的人生。

语言点例释

1. 实际上，我们现在能摸的青羊是现代人模仿文物做成的，样子虽然一模一样，但是比文物要大得多。

"模仿"是一个动词，意思是"照着某种现成的样子学着做"，例如"小孩儿总爱模仿大人的动作"。

2. 根据民间传说，这一天是百花仙子的生日，人们称之为"花朝节"。

"根据"在这句话中是一个介词，表示方式，意思是"以某种事物作为结论的前提或语言行动的基础"，例如"学校根据学生的中文水平分班"；"根据大家的意见，我们修改了计划"。

读后思考

1. 青羊宫是哪种宗教的庙宇？
2. 为什么人们都喜欢去摸青羊宫里的青羊雕像？

交流讨论

根据自己的了解，和同学讨论并分析佛教和道教思想的联系与区别。

亲身体验

请阅读以下《道德经》中的名句，通过查阅资料理解其中的内涵。

道可道，非常道；名可名，非常名。

人法地，地法天，天法道，道法自然。

善有果而已，不敢以取强。

(4) Qingyang Palace: Representative of Taoism

Taoism is one of the most important religions in China, which has its origins in this country from the earliest times. It started in the Sichuan region during the Eastern Han Dynasty, and then spread to the

古迹篇
Historical Sites

rest of China. Therefore, Taoism remains closely connected to Sichuan culture, and many Taoist temples have been established in Sichuan, among which the most famous one is Qingyang Palace (also known as Qingyang Temple or Green/Black Goat Temple).

Firstly, why is it called Qingyang? Legend has it that there was a man who was listening to Lao Tzu preaching his *Tao Te Ching*. In the middle of the lecture, since Lao Tzu had to leave for some business, the man was told to come to the Qingyang Market in Chengdu sometime later. Afterwards, Lao Tzu did finish preaching *Tao Te Ching* at the Qingyang Market, where a kind of green-black colored goat was bought and sold. Later, Lao Tzu was revered as the founder of Taoism and *Tao Te Ching* was regarded as one of its central texts. Therefore, people established a Taoist temple here at the market, named Qingyang Temple, based on this story.

Then in the Tang Dynasty, an emperor passed by Chengdu and stayed at Qingyang Temple. After he returned to the capital, he sent a lot of money to thank the Taoist priests for their hospitality. The Taoist priests used the money to expand the temple, and renamed it Qingyang Palace, signifying that it was a temple where the emperor had stayed. As a result, Qingyang Palace became one of the most influential Taoist sites in the Tang Dynasty.

The most famous artifacts at Qingyang Palace are the two bronze statues of black goats, donated by two Taoists in the Qing Dynasty. On the left is a single-horned black goat, while on the right side is a double-horned one. The one on the left is especially interesting as it blends

together the characteristics of the twelve Chinese Zodiac, including the ears of a rat, the body of an ox, the claws of a tiger, the back of a rabbit, the horns of a dragon, the tail of a snake, the mouth of a horse, the beard of a goat, the head of a monkey, the eyes of a rooster, the belly of a dog, and the butt of a pig. According to folklore, people back then believed that this was a magical goat, which could heal the pain in one's body by being touched the same part. That's why the goat statue has become so shiny from visitors' touches. But in fact, the goat statue that can be touched now is just a modern replica, much bigger than the original one even if looking alike. As for the authentic artifacts, one can appreciate them at the exhibition hall at Qingyang Palace.

On every 15th day of the second lunar month, Qingyang Flower Fair is held in this temple, because the folklore goes that this day is the birthday of the Flower Fairy. Additionally, this day is considered to be Lao Tzu's birthday by Taoism, thus since the Tang Dynasty, religious activities have been conducted every year. Attending Qingyang Flower Fair is one of the most famous traditional customs in Chengdu. On this day, Taoists, of course, usually arrive at the temple very early to commemorate Lao Tzu's birthday, while non-Taoists come to appreciate the beautiful flowers, taste the street food, and enjoy the early spring. In ancient times, the fair lasted for one month to create a grand celebration of spring. Although it typically does not last that long nowadays, people's enthusiasm for participating in the fair stills remains high. Like other religious sites in Sichuan, the Qingyang Palace harmoniously connects religion with secular life, making the believers and non-

古迹篇
Historical Sites

believers to exchange with each other and to enjoy beautiful Sichuan together.

> **Notes**
>
> 1. 实际上，我们现在能摸的青羊是现代人模仿文物做成的，样子虽然一模一样，但是比文物要大得多。
>   "模仿" is a verb which means "to imitate". For example:
>   小孩儿总爱模仿大人的动作。
> 2. 根据民间传说，这一天是百花仙子的生日，人们称之为"花朝节"。
>   "根据" in this sentence is a preposition used to mean "on the basis of, according to". For example:
>   学校根据学生的中文水平分班。
>   根据大家的意见，我们修改了计划。

Questions

1. What religion does Qingyang Temple serve?

2. Why do people like to touch the two statues of black goats in Qingyang Temple?

Discussion

Please discuss and analyze the similarities and differences between Buddhism and Taoism with others.

Experience

Please read the following famous sentences from *Tao Te Ching* and try to understand the meaning.

道可道，非常道；名可名，非常名。

人法地，地法天，天法道，道法自然。

善有果而已，不敢以取强。

六、人物篇

文物古迹固然令人惊叹，鲜活的人物似乎更能体现四川历史中的光荣与苦难。本篇和你一起追忆那些出生或是生活在四川的古代名人。

6. People

While the cultural relics and historical sites indeed awe-inspiring, the living personalities seem to better embody the glories and hardships in the history of Sichuan. Here is a glance at the ancient celebrities who were born or lived in Sichuan in this chapter.

第二眼看：
向世界讲述四川故事
Second Glance at Sichuan: Telling Sichuan Stories to the World

（一）政治双星

你一定听说过中国唯一一位女皇帝武则天吧？那你知道武则天是四川人吗？是的，她出生在今天的四川省广元市。武则天生活在中国的唐朝时期，开始是帮助皇帝管理国家，后来在自己67岁时终于当上了皇帝。武则天作为皇帝，既聪明又努力，特别善于任用人才来管理国家。她在当时制定了很多政策，对国家产生了很好的影响。现在，人们仍然非常欣赏她的一些政策，例如制定了更公平的国家考试制度，使来自不同背景的人才能为国家工作；再如严格惩罚腐败行为，奖励清正的官员，鼓励官员对皇帝和政府提意见，而且会尽量采纳这些意见。同时，她还在经济上减少税收，促进了农业生产。还值得一提的是，武则天加强了陆上和海上的丝绸之路，使中国和东南亚、南亚、中亚的国家连接在了一起。

在中国古代的男权社会中，武则天的经历可以说是女性非常成功的案例，很有传奇色彩。直到现在，还有很多小说、电影和电视剧都是根据她的生活改编而成。四川省广元市还保留着武则天的祠堂——皇泽寺。里面有国内唯一一座武则天的真容石刻像，也就是说这座石刻像展现的是她真实的容貌。整座石像是用整块石头雕刻成的，高达1.8米。如果仔细看还能发现，石像的武则天穿的不是皇帝的衣服，而是僧尼的袍子。这是因为武则天一生都信仰佛教。

下面说到的这位，也是著名的政治人物，却是一颗煞星。他不是四川人，但给四川人带来了巨大的痛苦和创伤。他就是张献忠，明朝末年的农民军领袖。他在明朝末年带领军队进入四川，建立了大西政权，都城就在成都。由于没有受过很好的教育，也

没有任何管理经验，张献忠对大西政权的领导很不顺利，政权很快就瓦解了。从进入四川到失败逃出四川，张献忠给四川造成了很大的破坏，也给四川人民带来了非常大的灾难。很多历史材料都描写到，张献忠的统治结束后，以前繁华的成都城市完全变了样子，大部分人被杀死，房屋被毁坏，附近森林里的野兽在白天也会跑到街道上来吃人。"天府之国"便就此衰败了。清朝初年，政府甚至不得不把很多人从中国其他地方转移到四川来生产和生活。可以说，现在的很多成都人其实都是来自别的地方的人的后代。

语言点例释

1. 再如严格惩罚腐败行为，奖励清正的官员，鼓励官员对皇帝和政府提意见，而且会尽量采纳这些意见。

"鼓励"是一个动词，意思是"用言语、文字等方法使某人或单位增强信心和决心"，例如"老师鼓励学生提出问题"。

2. 如果仔细看还能发现，石像的武则天穿的不是皇帝的衣服，而是僧尼的袍子。

"不是……而是……"连接两个分句，表示否定前者、肯定后者，例如"这不是我的书，而是他的"；"我不是不想去，而是没时间"。

拓展阅读

煞星

煞星，本来是阴阳学中的术语，后来常常比喻极为暴恶的人。

读后思考

1. 中国有很多电视剧都以武则天的历史故事为蓝本，你认为她的故事为什么如此受欢迎？

2. 张献忠的统治时代是四川历史上最黑暗的时期之一，问问你的四川朋友，他们是怎么看待这段历史的？

Second Glance at Sichuan: Telling Sichuan Stories to the World

交流讨论

你还知道中国哪些著名的政治家，请和同伴交流、分享。

名字	年代	著名事迹

(1) Two Political Figures

One must have heard of Wu Zetian, the only empress in the history of China. But does anyone know that she was from Sichuan? As a matter of fact, Wu was born in present-day Guangyuan city, Sichuan province, and lived during the Tang Dynasty. At first, she helped the emperor in governing the country, and later, at the age of 67, she officially became the empress herself. As an empress, Wu Zetian was both intelligent and diligent, particularly skilled at appointing talented individuals to govern the country. She issued plenty of policies at that time, positively affecting the country, many of which have been greatly admired even nowadays. For example, she launched a much fairer national examination system, allowing talents from different backgrounds to access government positions. Meanwhile, she also punished corruption severely, rewarded upright officials, and encouraged officials to express their opinions on herself and the government, making efforts to adopt those opinions. Furthermore, she reduced taxes and promoted agricultural production, thus contributing to the economy. Most notably, she strengthened of the functions of the Silk Road, both overland and maritime, connecting China with countries in Southeast Asia, South

Asia, and Central Asia.

In that patriarchal society of ancient China, Wu Zetian's journey can be considered highly successful and legendary. Even now, many novels, movies and TV drama series have been adapted from her life. Now, the Huangze Temple, serving as her ancestral hall, is still preserved in Guangyuan city. Inside the temple, there is the only authentic stone carving of Wu Zetian's likeness across the country, depicting her true appearance. The entire statue, carved from a single stone block, is 1.8 meters high. Upon closer examination, one can notice that Wu is depicted wearing the robes of a Buddhist nun rather than imperial clothing. This is because she embraced Buddhism throughout her life.

The next figure is also a famous political figures, who, however, is known as a malevolent star. He was not from Sichuan but brought great pains and traumas to Sichuan people. His name is Zhang Xianzhong, a peasant rebel leader in the late Ming Dynasty. In the final years of the Ming Dynasty, he led his army into Sichuan and established the Daxi regime with Chengdu as the capital city. Due to the lack of proper education and management experience, Zhang Xianzhong's leadership of the Daxi regime faced numerous difficulties and quickly ended in failure. From his entry into Sichuan to his eventual escape, Zhang caused significant destruction and brought tremendous disaster to Sichuan people. According to many historical records, following the downfall of his rule, the previously prosperous Chengdu underwent a complete transformation: most people were killed, houses were

第二眼看四川
向世界讲述四川故事
Second Glance at Sichuan: Telling Sichuan Stories to the World

vandalized, and wild animals from the nearby forests roamed on the streets to attack people even during daylight. From then on, the "Land of Abundance" fell into decline. During the early years of the Qing Dynasty, the government had to relocate many people from other parts of China to Sichuan for production and livelihood. It can be said that the current residents of Chengdu are mostly migrants from elsewhere.

Notes

1. 再如严格惩罚腐败行为，奖励清正的官员，鼓励官员对皇帝和政府提意见，而且尽量采纳这些意见。

"鼓励" is a verb which means "to encourage". For example:
老师鼓励学生提出问题。

2. 如果仔细看还能发现，石像的武则天穿的不是皇帝的衣服，而是僧尼的袍子。

"不是……而是……" connects two clauses, indicating the negation of the former and the confirmation of the latter. For example:
这不是我的书，而是他的。
我不是不想去，而是没时间。

Extensive Reading

煞星 (shàxīng)

The word "煞星" literally means malevolent star, originating from the Chinese philosophy of Yin and Yang. It is often used metaphorically to describe someone who is extremely violent and evil.

Questions

1. Why do you think that so many TV drama series are based on the historical stories of Wu Zetian? Why are her stories so popular?

2. Zhang Xianzhong's rule is one of the darkest periods in the history of Sichuan. Ask your friends from Sichuan about their opinions on his period of history.

人物篇
People

◎ **Discussion** ◎

Do you know any other famous statesmen in ancient China? Discuss and share with others.

Name	Historical Period	Story

（二）治水双星

由于气候湿润，河流众多，古代的四川地区是一个常常发生水患的地方，甚至有"泽国"的别名。"泽"就是水的意思，"泽国"意思是有很多水的地方。因此，四川历史上出现了很多带领大家一起治理水患的大英雄。其中最著名的两位是大禹和李冰。

大禹是中国历史上第一个真正意义上的国家——夏的第一个国王。他可不姓"大"，"大"是因为人们尊敬他，所以在他的名字前加上了尊称，即"伟大的禹"。传说，大禹的爸爸叫鲧。鲧接受了当时国王安排的任务，要治理水患。在治理的过程中，鲧始终使用堵水的方法，在河的两岸修建河堤，防止水流到河岸边的村子里。但是这样一来，如果雨越下越久，河水越来越高，那河堤也就越修越高，而河水一旦突破了河堤，就会冲毁更多的村庄。就这样，鲧治理了9年也没有成功，最后被国王杀掉了。大禹继续父亲的工作，充分总结了这些工作的经验和教训。他换了一种方法，叫作疏导法，就是利用水总是向低处流的规律，疏通各处水道，把洪水引到大海里。这样一来，水患就彻底消除了。大禹治水一开始是在四川地区，后来因为有了成功的经验，就渐渐地把疏导法推广到了其他地方。在治水的过程中，大禹到过很多地方，包括今天的山西、河南、安徽等地区，了解了各地的具

· 153 ·

第二眼看：
向世界讲述四川故事
Second Glance at Sichuan: Telling Sichuan Stories to the World

体情况，并且根据这些情况制定了很多好的政策，从而得到了人们的信任。因此，当时的国王在临死时让大禹继承了自己的王位。大禹从此建立了中国第一个世袭制朝代。世袭制的意思是如果爸爸是国王，那么他死了以后会把王位传给自己的儿子。因为治水的功绩，大禹在道教中被尊为水官大帝，生日是十月十五日，也就是中国古代的下元节。

李冰曾经是秦国负责管理四川地区的官员。在工作期间，他和自己的儿子一起领导人们修建了很多水利工程，其中包括著名的都江堰水利工程。当时李冰来到四川，发现水患严重，于是不久后就开始进行大规模的治水工作。李冰父子继承了大禹的疏导法，通过实地考察，找到最好的引水口和出水口；同时还创新地建立了分水坝，就是将河流分为两股，以减少出水的压力。在修建分水坝时，李冰让大家先做好大竹笼，装满石头，然后一个一个地沉到水底，终于在急流中建好了水坝。这一方法不仅产生了很好的效果，还充分利用了四川的特产——竹编，成本很低。后来的人认为这一方法很好地体现了道家的"道法自然""天人合一"的思想，是一种很值得学习的做事情的思路。从此以后，成都平原的农业生产有了保证，成为天下的粮仓，获得了"天府之国"的美称。在修完都江堰之后，李冰又到了四川别的地方修建水利设施，直到病死在工作中。为了纪念他，人们不仅为他修建了"二王庙"，还尊称他为"川主"。

人物篇
People

语言点例释

1. 这样一来，水患就彻底消除了。

"这样一来"表示承接上文所说的这种情况，表示前面出现了某种情况，带来了后面所说的结果，多用于口语，例如"他听了医生的话，每天都去外面散步，这样一来，他的病很快就好了"。

2. 因此，当时的国王在临死时让大禹继承了自己的王位。

"继承"是一个动词，在这句话中的意思是"按照法律或遗嘱接受死者的财产、职务、地位等"，例如"继承家业，继承财产"。"继承"还有"继续做前人未完成的事业，把前人留下的财富、传统、事业接受过来，使其延续下去"的意思，例如"我们要继承和发扬前辈们的奋斗精神"。

读后思考

1. 为什么治水在古代四川有特别重要的价值和意义？

2. 你参观过都江堰吗？请根据相关资料了解都江堰的治水原理。

交流讨论

大禹、李冰，还有我们以前谈到过的诸葛亮都是四川人民乃至中国人民最尊敬和怀念的人。你能总结出他们在做人做事方面的共同点吗？

(2) Two Stars of Flood Control and Management

With its humid climate and numerous rivers, the ancient Sichuan was a place of frequent floods, even earning it the name of "泽国 (Zéguó)" which means a place with abundant water. Therefore, in the ancient history of Sichuan, there emerged many great heroes who led people to control water disasters, among whom the most well-known two are Yu the Great ["大禹 (Dà Yǔ)"] and Li Bing.

Second Glance at Sichuan: Telling Sichuan Stories to the World

Yu the Great, or Great Yu, was the first king of Xia Dynasty which inaugurated dynastic rule in China. The title "Great" was added as a respectful prefix to his name because he was highly esteemed by the people.

According to several legends, Yu's father, Gun, was tasked with devising a system to control the flooding by the king of that time. Gun spent more than nine years building a series of dikes and dams along the riverbanks to prevent water from pouring into the villages, but all of his efforts were ineffective. Because of the continuous heavy rainfall and the rising water levels, the dikes finally collapsed, devastating even more villages. As a result, Gun was executed by the king due to his failure. Yu continued his father's work, and drew on the experience and lessons learned from it. Yu adopted a different method that is to dredge the riverbeds by making use of water naturally flowing towards lower areas to relieve floodwater into the ocean. Thus, this method effectively eliminated water disasters. Yu initially focused on water management in Sichuan but later expanded the use of the diversion method to other areas due to its success. With his water management efforts, Yu traveled to many places at that time, including present-day Shanxi, Henan, Anhui and so on. He gained a comprehensive understanding of local conditions and put forward numerous effective policies, earning the trust and respect of the people. Therefore, the king at that time passed the throne to Yu instead of his own son. Yu established Xia Dynasty (2070 BC–1600 BC), the first hereditary dynasty in China, which means the succession in control of a country is passed from father to son.

人物篇
People

Because of his great achievements in flood control, Yu was honored as the Emperor of Water in Taoism. His birthday was on the 15th day of the tenth lunar month, which was known as the Xia-Yuan Festival in ancient China.

Another star is Li Bing who served the state of Qin as an administrator in charge of Sichuan. During his tenure, Li Bing and his son helped people construct many water conservancy projects, including the famous Dujiangyan Irrigation System. At that time, Li Bing came to Sichuan and witnessed the severe floods, so he initiated large-scaled water-control projects immediately. Li Bing and his son followed the dredging method pioneered by Yu the Great and identified the best locations for water inlets and outlets through field investigations. Meanwhile, a water-diversion levee was built innovatively, diverting the river into two branches to reduce the hydraulic pressure. During the construction of the levee, Li Bing asked workers to make large baskets of woven bamboo filled with stones, then drop them into the river one by one, and eventually, the levee was built in the swift torrent. This method not only worked perfectly, but also took full advantage of the Bamboo Weaving, a local specialty of Sichuan, resulting in low construction costs. Later generations believed that this method embodied the thoughts of Taoism, including "Everything follows the laws of nature" and "Man is an integral part of nature", which became a valuable approach to work. Since then, the agricultural production of the Chengdu Plain has been ensured, gaining the reputation as the "Land of Abundance" and the granary of the world. After the completion of the Dujiangyan Irrigation System, Li Bing continued to extend his water management efforts to other parts of Sichuan until he died of illness at work. In memory of him, people not only built the "Two Kings Temple", but also revered him as the "River God".

Notes

1. 这样一来，水患就彻底消除了。

"这样一来" means "as thus". For example:

他听了医生的话，每天都去外面散步，这样一来，他的病很快就好了。

2. 因此，当时的国王在临死时让大禹继承了自己的王位。

"继承" is a verb which means "to inherit". For example:

继承家业/继承财产。

"继承" also means "to carry on what predecessors left off". For example:

我们要继承和发扬前辈们的奋斗精神。

Questions

1. Why was flood control and management of great value and significance in ancient Sichuan?

2. Have you ever visited Dujiangyan? Please learn about the flood control principles of Dujiangyan Irrigation System.

Discussion

Yu the Great, Li Bing, and Zhuge Liang, are the most respected and revered figures among the people of Sichuan and even the people of China. Please try to summarize their similarities in terms of character and accomplishments.

（三）文学双星

下面这两位川籍文学家，在中国可以说是家喻户晓。

人物篇
People

如果你去问中国朋友：你认为西方最伟大的文学家是谁？只能说一位。他多半会说莎士比亚。如果你再问，那中国呢？还是只能说一位，他多半会说李白。是的，虽然在文学界很难说出谁是第一名，但是李白在中国人的心目中就是有第一的地位。说得夸张一点儿，每个中国人会背的第一首唐诗，一定是李白写的《静夜思》，而几乎每个中国人都能背出至少一句李白的诗句。说到夸张，不管是李白的诗，还是李白的人生，都美得夸张。

李白，好写诗，好剑术，好旅游，好交友，好喝酒。是不是很符合我们对诗人的想象？实际上，早在他生活的唐朝，身边的人就对他崇拜得不得了，称他为"谪仙人"，意思就是来到人间的神仙。李白从十几岁开始四处游历，看遍大好的风景，一边交友，一边写诗。他写四川风景是"连峰去天不盈尺"，意思是连续的山峰离天不过一点点距离；他写和朋友的感情是"浮云游子意，落日故人情"，意思是云和太阳都在表达自己的深情；他写自己是"天生我材必有用"，意思是自己就是天才，肯定会有成功的一天……李白的诗充满了浪漫的感情，读起来特别爽快，能够引起人们特别是年轻人的共情。难怪从古到今，人们一直那么喜欢他，称他为写诗的神仙——"诗仙"。

与李白一样，苏轼同样是从古到今的实力派"流量明星"[1]。苏轼生活在北宋时期，是著名的文学家、书法家和画家。首先说文学。每年中秋节，中国中央电视台都有一台中秋晚会。要知道，看晚会的电视直播可是很多中国人过节的传统。而每年的中秋晚会，必然出现一首宋词——《水调歌头·明月几时有》。说

---

1 "流量明星"是一个网络用语，其中的"流量"指的是网站的访问量，也就是说有些明星能够吸引大家到网站上去关注他们，受到大家的广泛欢迎。

第二眼看四川：
向世界讲述四川故事
Second Glance at Sichuan: Telling Sichuan Stories to the World

实话，这真的会让晚会导演感到为难，一方面，如果不出现这首词，中国的观众肯定是不答应的；但另一方面，每年都要以新的表演形式来展示这首词，真的很困难啊！那么这首词到底有什么魅力呢？我们只说其中一句，"但愿人长久，千里共婵娟"，意思是：只希望大家都能好好生活，虽然离得很远，也能够共同享受这美好的月光。这正是中秋节的意义啊！文学的一大价值就在于能表达出我们能够切身感受到却不一定能够说出来的情感，让我们充满被理解的快乐。

巧的是，苏轼和李白一样都信仰道教，一样是浪漫而有趣的人。当在生活中遇到不顺利，苏轼说"小舟从此逝，江海寄余生"，希望自己乘坐的小船就这样漂走，剩下的日子都在江和海上度过；当怀念自己去世的妻子，他说"十年生死两茫茫，不思量，自难忘"，虽然过了十年，虽然不是刻意想起，但是却从来不会忘记那段深情。

值得一提的是，苏轼的父亲、弟弟都是很优秀的文学家。现在四川省眉山市还有他们的故居——"三苏祠"。门口写着"一家三父子，都是大文豪；诗赋传千古，峨眉共比高"[1]。

三苏祠

---

1 大意是这家父子三人都是伟大的文学家，才华就好像峨眉山一样高。

语言点例释

1. 说到夸张，不管是李白的诗，还是李白的人生都美得夸张。

"不管……，都/也……"表示条件，意思是"虽然条件不同，但是做法不变"，例如"不管明天是否下雨，我都要去看他"；"不管有多难，我也会坚持学下去"。需要注意的是，"不管"后面一定要有疑问代词或并列词组，例如"不管我们谁有困难，他都热情帮助"；"不管白天黑夜，医院里都有医生"。

2. 实际上，早在他生活的唐朝，身边的人就对他崇拜得不得了，称他为"谪仙人"，意思就是来到人间的神仙。

这句话的大意是"唐朝时，身边的人就很崇拜李白"。其中"崇拜"是动词，意思是"尊敬佩服"，例如"崇拜英雄，崇拜老师"。

拓展阅读

三苏祠

"三苏祠"，也就是苏洵、苏轼、苏辙的故居，位于四川省眉山市。不过我们现在看到的这些建筑是清代重新修建的，体现了清代园林的特色。

读后思考

1. 通过李白的诗句，你觉得他的性格特点是怎样的？

2. 你觉得为什么中国人那么喜欢苏轼这首关于中秋节的《水调歌头·明月几时有》？

亲身体验

四川眉山有一道特色菜——东坡肘子，请你上网查一查这道菜和苏东坡有什么关系。有机会的话，一定要亲口品尝一下哦！

(3) Two Literary Stars

The following two literary figures from Sichuan are widely known throughout China.

Second Glance at Sichuan: Telling Sichuan Stories to the World

Nearly all the Chinese people, if asked "Who do you think is the greatest Western literary figure?", would most likely mention Shakespeare. And if it is asked about the Chinese counterpart, their answer must be Li Bai. Indeed, while it is difficult to determine a definitive ranking in the literary world, Li Bai holds a special place in the hearts of the Chinese people. To some extent, the first Tang poem that every Chinese person can recite must be Li Bai's "Quiet Night Thought", and nearly every Chinese person can effortlessly quote at least one verse of Li Bai's poems. In fact, not only his poetry but also his life is extremely beautiful.

Li Bai was indeed a poet who embodied many qualities that align with one's imagination of a poet. He excelled in poetry, Chinese swordsmanship, traveling, making friends, and drinking. In fact, during his lifetime in the Tang Dynasty, people around him admired him so much that they called him "Banished Transcendent", signifying a celestial being who had descended to the mortal realm.

Li Bai has been traveling since he was a teenager, enjoying the spectacular landscapes, making friends, and writing poetry. His descriptions of Sichuan's landscapes include lines like "A chain of peaks stretching to the sky, less than a foot away", indicating the mountains are remarkably high. His portrayal of friendship can be seen in lines such as "Drifting clouds echo the wanderer's thoughts, the setting sun reflects an old friend's feelings", with both the clouds and the sun expressing his deep feelings. He also expressed his self-confidence in lines like "Heaven has made us talents, we're not made

in vain", implying that he possessed innate genius and would inevitably achieve success. Thus, it can be seen that Li Bai's poems are full of romantic feelings, which, therefore, can resonate with readers, especially the young people. No wonder people, since the ancient times, have been so fond of him, referring to him as the "Immortal Poet", a celestial being in the realm of poetry.

Similar to Li Bai, Su Shi was also a prominent "internet celebrity" from ancient to modern times. Su Shi, also known as Su Dongpo, was a renowned literary figure, calligrapher and painter during the Northern Song Dynasty. Above all, Su's literary contributions. Every year, China Central Television (CCTV) holds a live Moon Festival Gala. And watching the live broadcast of this gala has become a tradition for many Chinese people. In this gala, a Song Ci (Song-Dynasty poetry) entitled "Shuidiao Getou", or "Tune: Prelude to Water Melody" is performed every year. Frankly speaking, on the one hand, the audiences would be definitely unhappy without this poem, but on the other hand, it must be quite challenging to present this poem in new performance formats each year. So, what makes this poem so charming? Just to pick one line of it: "May we all be blessed with longevity and happiness, even though being thousands of miles apart, we are still able to share the beauty of the moon together." This is exactly the essence of the Moon Festival. One of the great values of literature is to express the feelings that one can deeply feel but cannot easily speak out, thus leaving people with the joy of being poetically understood.

Interestingly, Li Bai and Su Shi both believed in Taoism and

possessed a romantic and intriguing personality. When faced with obstacles and hardships, Su Shi said, "If I could only just disappear on a little boat, among rivers and seas for the rest of my life from here on"; when he missed his late wife, he thought "Ten years parted, one living, one dead; Not thinking, yet never forgetting". Despite the passing of ten years and not deliberately recalling the memories, that deep affection remains unforgettable.

It is worth noting that Su Shi's father and younger brother were also excellent literary figures, and their former residence Sansu Memorial Temple can still be found in Meishan city, Sichuan province. The entrance is inscribed with the words, "Three men in the Su family, all are great literary giants; Their poetry will remain forever, up to the summit of Mount Emei"[1].

---

1 The main idea is that all three of them are great writers whose talents are as high as Mount Emei.

人物篇
People

Notes

1. 说到夸张，不管是李白的诗，还是李白的人生都美得夸张。

"不管……，都/也……" indicates conditional relation, which means "the ways of doing something remain the same although conditions vary". For example:

不管明天是否下雨，我都要去看他。

不管有多难，我也会坚持学下去。

"不管" must be followed by an interrogative pronoun or coordinative phrase. For example:

不管我们谁有困难，他都热情帮助。

不管白天黑夜，医院里都有医生。

2. 实际上，早在他生活的唐朝，身边的人就对他崇拜得不得了，称他为"谪仙人"，意思就是来到人间的神仙。

This sentence basically means "唐朝时，身边的人就很崇拜李白". Here, "崇拜" is a verb which means "to adore, to worship". For example:

崇拜英雄 / 崇拜老师。

Extensive Reading

Sansu Memorial Temple

Sansu Memorial Temple, the former residence of Su Xun, Su Shi and Su Zhe, is located in Meishan city, Sichuan province. But the buildings we see today are blended with characteristics of gardens in the Qing Dynasty when they were reconstructed.

Questions

1. What do you think of Li Bai's character through his poems?

2. Why do you think that Chinese people are so fond of Su Shi's "Shuidiao Getou" about the Moon Festival?

Experience

In Meishan of Sichuan province, there is a special dish named Dongpo Pig Knuckle ["东坡肘子 (Dōngpō Zhǒuzi)" in Chinese].

· 165 ·

Please search online to find out its relations with Su Shi. If chances come, don't hesitate to taste it!

（四）科学双星

与前三节我们提到的人物相比，科学家们的名气似乎寂寞一点儿。但是下面我们要谈到的两位四川籍科学家，只要提到他们的贡献，你一定会说："啊！原来是他发明（发现）的？！"

第一位科学家被誉为"春节老人"。没错，正是他确立了以正月为一年的开始。这也就是春节的来历。这位科学家名字叫落下闳，姓落下，名闳。当时，中国处于汉朝，民间使用的历法有很多错误。这时，落下闳开始了修改历法的工作。经过努力，他和同事们一起制定出了《太初历》。《太初历》按照春、夏、秋、冬的顺序确定时间节点，与农业生产的春种、秋收、夏忙、冬闲的节奏和季节变化的顺序相配合，方便了人们的生活，直到现在中国人还会根据节气来感知气候变化。除此之外，落下闳还提出了"浑天说"。他认为整个天地好像一个巨大的蛋，天是蛋壳，地是蛋黄。大家看，在2000多年前，这是不是一个很有想象力的观点？2004年，中国科学院天文台将自己发现的一颗小行星命名为"落下闳星"，以纪念这位杰出的天文学家。

除了科学方面的成就，落下闳最受后来的人们赞赏的是他的科学家品质。首先，他对科学有最纯粹的爱。在四川老家，落下闳的工作没有受到政府的支持，但他仍然坚持科学研究。他对天象的观察和记录成为后来制定《太初历》的基础。在制定出历法后，当时的皇帝非常高兴，想让落下闳做官。但是落下闳却拒绝

了，回到自己的家乡——四川阆中，继续自己的研究，并且培养了一大批天文学人才，使这座小城居然成为当时著名的天文研究中心。其次是他对科学踏实的追求。为了更准确地观察天文现象，落下闳在蟠龙山建立了我国最早的民间观星台；为了将天文观测和自己的宇宙理论相结合，他还制作了观测仪器——浑天仪。虽然这些仪器没能保留下来，但是其研究精神与方法使他无愧于科学家的美名。

浑天仪复原模型

　　第二位科学之星可以说是一位地理学家，也可以说是一位历史学家。之所以介绍他，是因为他的著作《华阳国志》具有特别重要的科学价值，是研究古代四川地理和历史情况都必须引用的一部书。他的名字叫常璩。这部书主要记录了从远古到东晋四川及周边地区的地理情况。例如，书中记录在汉朝，四川就发现了天然气。当时的人们称之为"火井"，因为把火扔到天然气井里，就会发出像雷一样的爆炸声。书中还提到，当时的人们用天然气来煮盐。这可是世界上使用天然气的最早记录。除了地理情况，书中还记录了历史上四川地区的政治发展情况和各类著名人物，第二眼看四川：
向世界讲述四川故事
Second Glance at Sichuan: Telling Sichuan Stories to the World

因此，这本书被认为是中国第一部方志，也就是第一部地方的历史书。

> **语言点例释**
>
> 1. 当时的皇帝非常高兴，想让落下闳做官。但是落下闳却拒绝了，回到自己的家乡——四川阆中，继续自己的研究。
>   这句话的大意是"落下闳拒绝了做官，回到了家乡"。其中"拒绝"是一个动词，意思是"不接受（请求、意见或赠礼等）"，例如"拒绝诱惑，遭到拒绝"。
> 2. 培养了一大批天文学人才。
>   "一大批"属于"数词+形容词+量词"结构，这种结构主要表达对量的大小的强调，含有一定的夸张意味。例如"一大杯茶，一长串葡萄，一小份米饭"。

读后思考

1. 在你看来，什么是"科学家品质"？为什么说落下闳身上表现出了这些品质？

2. 为什么说《华阳国志》既是一部历史书，又是一部地理学著作？

交流讨论

在你的国家有哪些伟大的古代科学家，他们做出了什么贡献？请和同伴一起分享、讨论。

科学家	生活的年代	伟大的贡献

(4) Two Scientific Stars

Compared with the figures mentioned in the previous sections, the scientists may not enjoy the same level of fame. However, as for

人物篇
People

the following two Sichuan-born scientists, once their remarkable contributions are introduced, one will definitely exclaim "Ah! It was invented (discovered) by them!"

The first scientist was honored as the "Elder of Spring Festival". That is because it was he who defined "正月 (zhēngyuè)" as the beginning of a lunar year. This is the origin of the Sping Festival. His name was Luoxia Hong, with Luoxia as his surname and Hong as his given name. During the Han Dynasty, there were many errors in the calendars used by the people. It was then that Luoxia Hong embarked on the task of revising the calendar. Through great efforts, he and his colleagues proposed "Taichu Calendar" (also called "Grand Inception"). This calendar divided a solar year into 24 solar terms based on the order of four seasons (spring-summer-fall-winter), aligning with the pace of agricultural activities such as sowing in spring, busy work in summer, harvest in autumn, and leisure in winter, which facilitated people's lives. Even today, Chinese people still perceive climate changes based on the solar terms derived from this calendar. In addition, Luoxia also put forward the "Celestial Sphere Theory", describing "the entire universe is like a huge egg, with the sky as the eggshell and the earth as the yolk". Isn't this a very imaginative idea over 2,000 years ago? In 2004, a small asteroid, discovered by National Astronomical Observatories affiliated with Chinese Academy of Science, was named after Luoxia Hong in commemoration of the outstanding Chinese astronomer.

In addition to his achievements, Luoxia Hong was mainly praised

for his qualities as a scientist. The first is his purest love for science. When he was in Sichuan, Luoxia Hong's work did not receive support from the government, but he still carried on scientific research. His observations and recordings of celestial phenomena laid the foundation for "Taichu Calendar". When the national calendar was established, the emperor at the time was extremely pleased and wanted Luoxia Hong to serve as an official. However, Luoxia Hong refused and returned to his hometown of Langzhong in Sichuan, continuing his research and cultivating a large number of talents in astronomy. As a result, this small city in Sichuan became a renowned center for astronomical research at that time. The second is his diligent pursuit of science. In order to observe astronomical phenomena more accurately, Luoxia Hong established one of China's earliest private observatory on Panlong mountain. For the sake of combining astronomical observations with his theory of the universe, he also invented an observer called Armillary Sphere. Although these instruments have not been preserved, his spirit and methods of research have earned him the esteemed title of a scientist.

The second scientist is arguably a geographer or a historian. The reason for selecting him as a scientific star is his book *Chronicles of Huayang* (or *Huayang Guo Zhi*), an extant gazetteer to study the geography and history of ancient Sichuan. His name is Chang Qu. This book mainly records the geographical situations of Sichuan and its surrounding areas from the ancient times to the Eastern Jin Dynasty. In

the case of the Han Dynasty, the book records the discovery of natural gas in Sichuan, which was called "fire well" at that time, because the sparks thrown into the gas well could cause an explosion like a thunder. It is also mentioned in the book that people used natural gas for salt production, making it the earliest known record of natural gas utilization in the world. In addition to geographical information, the book also documents the political development and various prominent figures in the history of Sichuan, so it is considered as China's first local history book.

Notes

1. 当时的皇帝非常高兴，想让落下闳做官。但是落下闳却拒绝了，回到自己的家乡——四川阆中，继续自己的研究。

    This sentence basically means "落下闳拒绝了做官，回到了家乡". Here, "拒绝" is a verb which means "to refuse". For example:

    拒绝诱惑 / 遭到拒绝

2. 培养了一大批天文学人才。

    The structure of "a number + an adjective + a measure word" such as "一大批" is mainly used to emphasize the size or the quantity of something with a bit of exaggeration. For example:

    一大杯茶 / 一长串葡萄 / 一小份米饭

Questions

1. In your opinion, what are the qualities of a scientist? Why do people think Luoxia Hong have such qualities?

2. Why is the *Chronicles of Huayang* considered both a history and a geography book?

第二眼看：

Second Glance at Sichuan: Telling Sichuan Stories to the World

Discussion

Are there any great scientists in your country? And what contributions did they make? Please share and discuss with others.

Scientist(s)	Historical Period(s)	Contributions

七、风物篇

个性鲜明的四川人做出来的东西自然与众不同。本篇为你介绍四种四川特产。

7. Specialties

The unique personalities of Sichuan people naturally reflect in the things and products they create. In this chapter, four distinctive specialties of Sichuan are introduced.

第二眼看四川：
向世界讲述四川故事
Second Glance at Sichuan: Telling Sichuan Stories to the World

（一）一杯茶，一段时光——川茶

在中国人看来，喝茶不能叫喝茶，要叫品茶。为什么叫品茶呢？你看这个"品"字，有三个口，就是三张嘴，一边喝茶，一边欣赏悠久的茶文化，一边慢慢享受与亲朋好友相聚的美好时光。所以来到中国，大家千万别错过那杯清香的茶，而要品茶，不妨尝尝来自四川的茗茶。

传统上，四川人最爱的是绿茶和花茶。绿茶是把摘下来的茶叶直接放到大铁锅里炒干，讲究茶叶的新鲜。每年初春，也就是中国的传统节日清明节前后，是茶叶最嫩最鲜的时候，茶农们开始采摘和制作绿茶。这时候的中国人都期待着"春茶上市"，等着尝尝春天的味道。人们每年都会早早去茶叶店预定新茶，好不容易等到了新茶上市，就会第一时间寄给在外地的亲朋好友们。再说花茶，花茶的制作比绿茶多了一个环节，就是把绿茶和茉莉花的香气融合。这个做法比较复杂，这里没有办法详细地说明，但是只要想想碧绿的茶叶和洁白的茉莉花在一起吐香的画面就已经能够感觉到很美了，对不对？

如果喜欢清香纯正的味道，那就来一杯"青城雪芽"或是"峨眉竹叶青"吧。这两种分别来自青城山和峨眉山的绿茶，应该盛放在玻璃杯里喝。这样可以看到碧绿的茶水中，一根根茶叶竖在杯中，好像茂密的森林。如果更爱浓厚丰富的口味，那么一定要尝尝茉莉花茶。在花茶中，茶叶的清香和茉莉花的淡雅融合在一起，喝一口就能让你忘记生活的烦恼，进入一个清新的美好世界。

花茶

点茶的时候,能微笑着把"竹叶青"或者"碧潭飘雪"这样的名字说出来,老板一定会视你为本地茶客;而如果能够说一句,"要今年的峨眉雪芽啊",老板就知道来的是品茶行家,必然奉上店里最好的茶。在四川这样一个茶文化悠久的地方,懂得品茶和欣赏茶绝对是一件值得骄傲的事情。

四川是中国茶的发源地之一。西汉时,住在成都的文学家王褒在对自己仆人的"工作要求"中写道:"烹茶尽具……武阳买茶"[1]。这篇文章是用和仆人开玩笑的语气写的,但是却在无意中留下了对古代人品茶生活的记录。"烹茶尽具"中的"烹"是煮的意思,"尽"是准备的意思,"具"指茶具,比如茶杯、茶壶,这句话的意思是煮好茶,并且准备好干净的茶具。"武阳买茶"中的"武阳"是一个地方的名字,在今天成都的附近,是古代有名的产茶地。我们可以看到,在那个时候,品茶就已经成为人们生活中的重要内容。实际上,这段文字已经被历史学家们认为是

---

[1] 参见王褒(西汉)所著《僮约》,载王洪林:《王褒集考译》,成都:巴蜀书社,1998,第14页。

第二眼看四川：
向世界讲述四川故事
Second Glance at Sichuan: Telling Sichuan Stories to the World

世界上最早的明确的关于喝茶的记录。另外，中国乃至世界上最早、最完整的茶文化专著——《茶经》则在书的最开始就说："茶者，南方之嘉木也。一尺、二尺乃至数十尺；其巴山峡川，有两人合抱者。"[1] 这里的"巴山峡川"大概就是指现在的四川和重庆地区。这句话的意思是说，茶是生长在南方的好树，高一尺、二尺或者几十尺。在四川和重庆地区，有的茶树很粗，需要两个人手拉手才能环抱。也就是说，自古以来，四川就被认为是中国茶的发源地。

语言点例释

1. 人们每年都会早早去茶叶店预定新茶，好不容易等到了新茶上市，就会第一时间寄给在外地的好朋友们。

　　"好容易"和"好不容易"都是很不容易的意思，常与副词"才"搭配使用，例如"我好（不）容易才通过了汉语水平考试"；"今天的作业太多了，好（不）容易才做完"。需要注意的是，"好（不）容易"只能用来叙述已经完成的事情或已经实现的愿望。

2. 这时候的中国人都会期待着"春茶上市"，等着尝尝春天的味道。

　　"期待"是一个动词，表示"对将来的某个时刻或者事物产生一种向往"，例如"他期待能够早点回家"；"我很期待圣诞节妈妈送给我的礼物"。

延伸阅读

四川名茶

　　"青城雪芽"和"峨眉竹叶青"是四川绿茶的两个品种名字，分别产自青城山和峨眉山。"碧潭飘雪"则是四川茉莉花茶的品种名字，是将竹叶青绿茶和茉莉花放在一起制作而成的。

读后思考

1. 你喝过中国茶吗？能用三个形容词来描述一下喝茶时的感

---

1 参见（唐）陆羽：《茶经》，南京：凤凰出版社，2007年，第1页。

受吗?

2.四川人所谓的"花茶"中的"花"指的是什么花?

亲身体验

尝一尝四川花茶和绿茶,说一说它们在色、香、味方面有何相同点与差异。

茶	闻一闻味道	看一看茶汤的颜色	品一品茶的味道
花茶			
绿茶			

交流讨论

在你的国家,人们爱喝茶吗?请查阅相关资料,聊一聊你的国家与中国的茶文化有哪些相似点,又有哪些不同点。

(1) Sichuan Tea: A Cup of Tea, a Taste of Time

From the Chinese people's perspective, drinking tea cannot be simply called "drinking tea", but "tasting tea" ["品茶 (pǐn chá)" in Chinese]. The character "品" is composed of three squares "口 (kǒu)" which indicate three mouths, signifying that while sipping the tea, one can also appreciate the profound tea culture and enjoy the delightful moments spent with family and friends. Thus, in China, one must never miss the fragrant Chinese tea, and if one would like to taste tea, why not try some Sichuan tea?

Green tea and jasmine tea have been the two favorites among Sichuan people since ancient times. As for green tea, the freshly picked tea leaves are pan-fried in a large iron wok, extracting the freshness of

Second Glance at Sichuan: Telling Sichuan Stories to the World

the tea. Every early spring, around the Tomb-sweeping Day, tea is at its freshest and tenderest condition, and that's when the tea farmers begin to pick and make green tea. At this time, people always eagerly await the "spring tea" coming into the market, anticipating the taste of spring. Many individuals make early reservations at tea shops every year for the new tea. After a lot of anticipation and patience, once they finally receive the new tea, they promptly send it to their friends who are living elsewhere. As for jasmine tea, its production involves an additional step of blending the fragrances of jasmine with tea, for example, the blend of jasmine and green tea. This process is rather complex and hard to elucidate in this text, but isn't it quite beautiful that the vibrant green tea leaves mingle with pure white jasmine blossoms while exuding their fragrance?

If one prefers a light and pure flavor, a cup of "Qingcheng Xueya" or "Emei Zhuyeqing" will be the best choice. These two green teas, originating from Mount Qingcheng and Mount Emei respectively, had better be served in a glass, as thus, one can see the tea leaves standing in the water like a flourishing forest. If one prefers a more robust and richer flavor, please do try the jasmine tea . It blends the delicate fragrance of green tea and the elegant flavor of jasmine flowers together. Just one sip can make people forget all the worries and transport to a refreshing and beautiful world.

When ordering tea in Sichuan, one will be surely considered a local tea enthusiast by saying tea names like "Zhuyeqing" or "Bitan Piaoxue" with a smile. And if one can even ask for the fresh Emei

风物篇
Specialties

Xueya of that year, they will undoubtedly be regarded as knowledgeable tea connoisseurs by the owner and be served with the best tea available in the shop. In Sichuan—a place with a long history of tea culture, it is highly valued to know how to properly taste and appreciate tea.

Sichuan is one of the birthplaces of Chinese tea. During the Western Han Dynasty, Wang Bao, a litterateur living in Chengdu, wrote in "The Servant's Contract" presenting an extended account of the onerous list of duties: "烹茶尽具 (pēng chá jìn jù)……武阳买茶 (Wǔyáng mǎi chá)". Although this article was an example of humorous writing, it unintentionally left a record of tea appreciation in ancient people's lives. In the first half of the sentence cited above, "烹" means "to boil", "尽" means "to prepare", "具" refers to tea utensils such as teacups and teapots, which means that the servants need to boil tea well and also prepare clean tea utensils. "武阳 (Wǔyáng)", a place near Chengdu, was well-known for tea production in ancient China. It is observed that tea-tasting had become a significant part of daily lives even at that time. Actually, historians have regarded this passage from Wang Bao as the earliest explicit record of tea-drinking throughout the world. Besides, in the beginning part of *The Classic of Tea*—the earliest and most comprehensive treatise on tea culture in China and even the whole world, it reads: "Tea, a fine and noble plant in southern regions, the height of which varies from one or two feet up to dozens of feet, depending on their habitat. The trunk of a kind of a gigantic arboreal tea plant found in Bashan and Xiachuan areas (east Chongqing and west Hubei province) can be encircled only by the

: 向世界讲述四川故事
Second Glance at Sichuan: Telling Sichuan Stories to the World

outstretched arms of two persons." In other words, since ancient times, Sichuan has been regarded as the birthplace of Chinese tea.

Notes

1. 人们每年都会早早去茶叶店预定新茶，好不容易等到新茶，就会第一时间寄给在外地的好朋友们。

"好容易" and "好不容易" both mean "with great difficulty" or "with much effort", and usually collocates with the adverb "才" ("only" or "finally"). For example:

我好（不）容易才通过了汉语水平考试。

今天的作业太多了，好（不）容易才做完。

It's important to note that "好（不）容易" is used to describe actions or desires that have already been accomplished or realized.

2. 这时候的中国人都会期待着"春茶上市"，等着尝尝春天的味道。

"期待" is a verb that means "to expect, to look forward to". For example:

他期待能够早点回家。

我很期待圣诞节妈妈送给我的礼物。

Extensive Reading

Famous Teas of Sichuan

"Qingcheng Xueya" and "Emei Zhuyeqing" are two kinds of green tea of Sichuan, produced in Mount Qingcheng and Mount Emei respectively. "Bitan Piaoxue" refers to a jasmine tea, which is made by mixing Zhuyeqing with jasmine flowers.

Questions

1. Have you ever tried Chinese tea? Please describe the tea taste with three adjectives.

2. What kind of flowers do Sichuan people use in herbal tea?

Experience

风物篇
Specialties

Try a cup of Sichuan herbal tea and green tea, and write down their similarities and differences in color, aroma and flavor.

Tea	Aroma	Color	Flavor
Herbal Tea			
Green Tea			

 **Discussion**

Do people like drinking tea in your home country? Please look up relevant materials and talk about the similarities and differences between the tea cultures in your home country and China.

（二）一段锦，一座城市——蜀锦

你记得成都还有个名字叫"锦官城"吗？去成都旅游的时候，你一定去过"锦里"吧？春天的时候，"锦江"旁的柳树冒着新绿，非常可爱……为什么成都有这么多的地方都以"锦"为名？

这里的"锦"指的是"蜀锦"。我们知道，"蜀"是四川地区在古代的名字。"锦"则是指有彩色花纹的丝绸，所以"蜀锦"的意思就是四川地区生产的一种丝绸。中国的丝绸一向闻名世界，而"蜀锦"则是最古老、最美丽的丝绸之一。今天的成都仍然被称为"锦官城"，意思是生产蜀锦的城市；城市里最有名的河叫作"锦江"，因为古代的织锦工人曾在那里洗蜀锦；外地的朋友来了，成都人总要请朋友去"锦里"喝喝茶，要知道现在这个繁华的旅游景点，古代曾是织锦工人们居住的地方。总之，蜀锦可是成都人的骄傲！当你看到"锦"这个字，不妨问问成都的朋友，看看这个地方是不是跟蜀锦有关系。

从古到今，人们最喜欢的是蜀锦上丰富而独特的花纹。这些

· 181 ·

第二眼看四川：向世界讲述四川故事
Second Glance at Sichuan: Telling Sichuan Stories to the World

花纹有花鸟、文字、景物、几何图案等。更有意思的是，这些花纹还有美好的寓意。例如，汉语中有一个成语，叫"锦上添花"，意思是好的情况还会更好。而蜀锦中也有一种华丽的花纹叫作"锦上添花"，是在小的花纹上再织上大花的图案——花上加花，希望大家好上加好！有的蜀锦还表现了中国独特的文化，例如有一种花纹是用流动的线条织出奔跑的动物，表示这些都是天上的动物，像云一样神秘。古代的人们受道教影响很大，他们认为天上的动物是吉祥的象征。所以，今天的我们能够在蜀锦上读到很多中国传统文化，特别是四川的地域文化。

每个时代对什么是"美"都有不同的观点，那么蜀锦为什么能一直得到人们的喜爱呢？那是因为时代在变，蜀锦也一直在变。在秦汉时，蜀锦有独特的民族特色；在唐代，蜀锦则有鲜明的色彩和丰富的花纹；到了宋代，蜀锦又变得朴素温柔；明清时，蜀锦则勇敢地学习了别的地方"锦"的花纹，创造出更新更美的图案。直到现在，蜀锦仍然受到人们的欢迎，常常被作为贵重的礼物送给亲朋好友。也许，这就是为什么蜀锦是四川文化的代表——精益求精和不断创新正是四川的精神！

蜀锦是中国"锦"的老师，这种说法可不是夸张！首先，蜀锦产生的时间最早，大约产生于两千多年前的战国时代，后来随着交通的发展，传到中国其他的地方；第二，蜀锦工艺影响了中国其他的"锦"，从考古的发现看来，几乎中国所有的"锦"都在技术和花纹方面受到了蜀锦的影响。

风物篇
Specialties

蜀锦的制作

现在的蜀锦是珍贵的艺术品，但在古代，人们在生活中用蜀锦做衣服、做被套等。三国时，蜀国的政府将蜀锦作为重要的经济来源，鼓励工人们生产蜀锦，卖到外地，甚至外国。我们都知道，瓷器、丝绸和茶叶是中国古代最有名的出口商品。事实上，在很长的历史时期，"丝绸"指的就是蜀锦。

唐代的诗人杜甫有一句很有名的诗，"晓看红湿处，花重锦官城"，意思是明天早上起床，一定会发现成都到处都是盛开的花朵。生活在花的城市中的人们，做出了蜀锦，比花更美的蜀锦则成为成都的象征。

第二眼看 ：
向世界讲述四川故事
Second Glance at Sichuan: Telling Sichuan Stories to the World

语言点例释

1. 中国的丝绸一向闻名世界，而"蜀锦"则是最古老、最美丽的丝绸之一。

"一向"表示从过去到现在，修饰表示持续的行为、状态的词语，例如"他一向不爱说话"。"一向"还可以作名词，例如"这一向你去哪儿了？"。

2. 在唐代，蜀锦则有鲜明的色彩和丰富的花纹。

"鲜明"是一个形容词，意思是"（颜色）清晰，明亮"，例如"他的画色彩鲜明，很受欢迎"。"鲜明"还有一个意思是"（态度、立场等）明确；不含糊"，例如"这篇论文的观点十分鲜明"。

读后思考

1. 你还知道成都哪些地方的名字里有"锦"吗？

2. 为什么说蜀锦是中国"锦"的老师？

交流讨论

2006年，蜀锦织造技艺被列入第一批国家级非物质文化遗产名录。不过对于年轻人来说，蜀锦离我们的生活很远。请和同伴讨论我们应该如何保护并传承这些传统工艺。

亲身体验

对蜀锦感兴趣的朋友可以前往成都市的蜀锦博物馆免费参观。这座博物馆中不仅陈列着蜀锦的产品，还有古代织造蜀锦机器的仿制品。

(2) Shu Jin: A Brocade, a City

Have you ever heard the expression of "Jinguan City"["锦官城(Jǐnguānchéng)" in Chinese]—a different name of Chengdu? When travelling in Chengdu, one must have been to the Jinli Street, right? In spring, the willows along the riversides of the Jinjiang River are fresh

风物篇
Specialties

green and very lovely. Why are there so many places in Chengdu with the word "Jin" in their names?

Here, the Chinese character "锦 (jǐn)" refers to "蜀锦 (Shǔ jǐn)" or the Sichaun Brocade. It is known that "Shu" is the name of Sichuan regions in ancient times, and "Jin" refers to the silk fabric with colorful patterns, so "Shu Jin" means a kind of silk fabric produced in Sichuan. China's silk products have always been renowned all over the world, and among those "Shu Jin" is one of the oldest and most beautiful. Today's Chengdu is still known as "Jinguan City", which means the city of Shu Brocade. The most famous river in the city is called "Jinjiang River" because the ancient weaving workers used to wash Shu Brocade there. Visitors are always invited by the Chengdu hosts to enjoy tea in the Jinli Street, the very bustling tourist attraction used to be the residence of the ancient Shu Brocade weaving workers. In short, Shu Jin is the pride of the Chengdu people! When seeing the character "锦", it is worth asking the friends from Chengdu to see if it has any connection to Shu Brocade.

From ancient times to the present, the various and unique patterns of Shu Jin, including flowers, birds, characters, landscapes, and geometric designs, are people's favorite. What is more fascinating is that these patterns also convey auspicious meanings. For example, there is a Chinese four-character idiom called "锦上添花 (jǐn shàng tiān huā)", which means to make a good situation even better. Meanwhile, Shu Jin has a magnificent pattern also called "锦上添花", involving big flowers on top of smaller patterns to symbolize the wish for continuous

prosperity. Some pieces of Shu Jin also showcase the uniqueness of the Chinese culture. For instance, there is a kind of pattern that uses flowing lines to depict running animals, symbolizing those animals are celestial creatures, as mysterious as clouds. This particular pattern reflects the strong influence of Taoism during that time, as people believed that celestial animals were auspicious symbols. Therefore, today when admiring Shu Brocade, one can see many traces of the traditional Chinese culture, particularly the regional culture of Sichuan.

Every era has its own perspective on what is considered "beauty", but Shu Brocade has continuously captured people's hearts, because it has evolved with the changing times. During the Qin and Han dynasties, Shu Jin showcased unique ethnic characteristics. In the Tang Dynasty, it featured vibrant colors and intricate patterns. During the Song Dynasty, the style of Shu Jin became more understated and much gentler. In the Ming and Qing dynasties, people created new and more beautiful patterns for Shu Jin by fearlessly borrowing from patterns of brocades elsewhere in China. Even nowadays, Shu Jin is still very popular across the nation, which is often presented as a valuable gift to families and friends. Perhaps this is why Shu Jin is the representative of Sichuan culture, since it embodies the spirit of constantly striving for excellence and innovation.

It is not an exaggeration to say that Shu Jin is the "master" of Chinese brocades. First, Shu Jin is the oldest brocade in China, which developed about two thousand years ago in the Warring States Period, and later, with the development of transportation, spread to other

parts of China. Second, according to archaeological discoveries, the craftsmanship of Shu Jin has influenced other Chinese brocades in the aspects of techniques and patterns.

Nowadays, Shu Jin is treasured as an art form. However, in ancient times, it was commonly used in daily life, such as for making clothes or quilts. In the Three Kingdoms Period , Shu Jin was recognized as an important economic resource by the government of the Shu state who encouraged workers to produce Shu Jin and sell it to other regions and even foreign countries. As is known to all that porcelain, silk, and tea were the most famous export items of ancient China. In fact, for a long period in history, the term "silk" referred specifically to Shu Jin.

There is a famous line by the Tang Dynasty poet Du Fu: "晓看红湿处，花重锦官城 (xiǎo kàn hóng shī chù, huā zhòng Jǐnguān chéng)", which means "Dawn sees saturated reds; The town's heavy with blooms". People living in this city of flowers created Shu Jin, a fabric even more beautiful than flowers, which has become a symbol of Chengdu.

: 向世界讲述四川故事
Second Glance at Sichuan: Telling Sichuan Stories to the World

🍀 Notes 🍀

1. 中国的丝绸一向闻名世界，而"蜀锦"则是最古老、最美丽的丝绸之一。

"一向" signifies a continuous action or state from the past to the present. It modifies words that represent ongoing behaviors or conditions. For example:

他一向不爱说话。

Additionally, "一向" can also function as a noun. For example:

这一向你去哪儿了？

2. 在唐代，蜀锦则有鲜明的色彩和丰富的花纹。

"鲜明" is an adjective in Chinese, meaning "vivid" or "bright" when describing colors. For example:

他的画色彩鲜明，很受欢迎。

Additionally, "鲜明" can also mean "clear" or "distinct" when referring to attitudes, positions, etc. For example:

这篇论文的观点十分鲜明。

🍀 Questions 🍀

1. Do you know any other places in Chengdu having names with "锦"?

2. Why is Shu Jin regarded as the "master" of Chinese brocades?

🍀 Discussion 🍀

In 2006, Shu Jin was listed in the first batch of National Intangible Cultural Heritage. But for the young people, Shu Jin is still far away from their daily lives. Please discuss how people can preserve and inherit these traditional crafts.

🍀 Experience 🍀

Those who are interested in Shu Jin can visit the Shu Jin Museum in Chengdu for free. The museum displays not only the products of Shu Jin but also replicas of ancient weaving machines used for producing it.

风物篇
Specialties

（三）一道菜，百种味道——川菜

四川地区的菜，即川菜，是中国传统四大菜系之一，也是当代中国最有特色、在民间最受欢迎的菜系之一。川菜以麻、辣、鲜、香为特色，以家常菜为主，所以又被中国人称为"百姓菜"。成都作为川菜的代表城市，在2010年被联合国教科文组织授予"世界美食之都"的称号。要知道，全世界只有6座城市获得了这个称号。可以说，川菜是四川最醒目的招牌之一。

在中国，如果你介绍自己是四川人，那周围的人多半会问，"那你很能吃辣哇？"而四川人也多半回答说，"是啊，无辣不欢！"意思是，没有辣椒，吃什么都没什么味道啊！辣，是川菜的一个主题词。传统川菜一直以"好辛香"为最大特点。这里的"辛"就是辣的意思。但在四川人看来，川菜真正的灵魂还在于把辣椒与黄豆进行的完美结合，也就是"豆瓣"。闻名全国的"郫县豆瓣"是四川人家家户户的必备，甚至在海外的很多超市也能买到。只要拿出"郫县豆瓣"，四川人便能迅速辨认出老乡，会马上用四川话招呼道，"四川哪儿的呢？"

郫县豆瓣

· 189 ·

第二眼看四川：
向世界讲述四川故事
Second Glance at Sichuan: Telling Sichuan Stories to the World

　　如果只是辣，四川菜的味道可能还没那么容易辨认。韩国菜、泰国菜、墨西哥菜等都各有各的辣法。四川的辣，是加上了花椒的麻辣，这一尝就很难让人忘记了。所以到了四川，一定要尝尝的菜品有麻婆豆腐、水煮肉片、夫妻肺片、辣子鸡丁等。如果尝了以后发现喜欢，那么祝贺你，对你来说，四川就是美食的天堂了！

麻婆豆腐

　　但是如果发现一开始不太适应，也别着急，新式川菜已经考虑过来自不同国家、不同地区朋友们的口味，讲究"一菜一格，百菜百味"。"百味"即一百种味道，这还真不是夸张！现在咱们吃到的川菜在麻、辣、甜、咸、酸、苦六种味道的基础上进行变化，组合成各种各样的味道。如果你暂时接受不了麻辣，完全没问题，请试着点一下：宫保鸡丁、鱼香肉丝、糖醋排骨、甜皮鸭等。总之，只要你走进川菜馆，就绝对不会失望的！

　　最后，但是绝对不是不重要的一个部分是四川的小吃。炎热的夏天，可以选一份川北凉粉，麻辣凉爽，最是提神；冬天不妨来一碗绵竹羊肉粉或是肥肠粉，温暖身心；下午4点想加餐，一两担担面最是合适，而喜欢甜食的朋友将面对赖汤圆、丁丁糖、

风物篇
Specialties

三大炮等,陷入选择困难;如果爱好"重口味",追求奇特的感受,就一定要试试怪味兔头、乐山钵钵鸡等特产。

话说有一位外国朋友,计划用三个月尝遍中国美食,然而三年过去了,他还在四川!当然,这只是网上的一个段子,是开玩笑的,实际的情况可能是,三年过去了,他都没有走出成都。

语言点例释

1. 只要拿出"郫县豆瓣",四川人便能迅速辨认出老乡。

"便"在这句话中是一个副词,与"如果、只要、既然"连用,表示上文的事实必然引出下文的结果或结论,例如"如果你来参加,他便也会来";"只要肯努力,便能成功";"既然大家不同意,便不要太勉强"。这里的"便"带有书面色彩。

2. 新式川菜已经考虑过来自不同国家、不同地区朋友们的口味。

"考虑"是一个动词,意思是"在做出决定前,进行思考",例如"我会认真考虑这个问题,然后回答你";"我们不能只考虑经济,不考虑环境"。

读后思考

1. 四川菜最有特色的味道是什么?你尝过吗?喜欢吗?

2. 有人说每个地方独特的饮食总是和这个地区的地理环境有关系,你觉得四川菜麻辣的特色会不会跟四川的自然环境有关呢?

交流讨论

对于四川人吃兔头、兔肉等现象,一部分外国朋友觉得很难接受,对此你怎么看?

亲身体验

"麻婆豆腐"里的"麻婆"是什么意思?"夫妻肺片"里的"夫妻"又指什么?请去川菜馆体验一下,找到答案,也可以寻找一些你感兴趣的菜名,理解其中的意思。

Second Glance at Sichuan: Telling Sichuan Stories to the World

(3) Sichuan Cuisine: One Dish, Countless Flavors

Sichuan cuisine, "川菜 (Chuāncài)" in Chinese, is one of the four traditional Chinese major culinary styles as well as one of the most distinctive and popular regional cuisines in today's China. Sichuan cuisine is characterized by its signature flavors of numbing and spicy, freshness, and aroma. It primarily consists of home-style dishes, so it is also called "common people's cuisine" by the Chinese people. Chengdu, as a representative city of Sichuan cuisine, was awarded the title of "City of Gastronomy" by UNESCO in 2010. It's worth noting that only six cities in the world have earned this honor. It can be said that Sichuan cuisine is one of the most eye-catching brands of Sichuan.

In China, if one introduces himself / herself as being from Sichuan, others will probably believe that this person must be good at eating spicy food. And most Sichuan people will reply, "Yes, we love spicy food! Without chili, nothing tastes good!" Spiciness is a key feature of Sichuan cuisine. Traditional Sichuan cuisine has always been characterized by its "spicy flavor" that is loved by the Sichuan people. However, for the Sichuan people, the true essence of Sichuan cuisine lies in the perfect combination of chili peppers and fermented soybeans, known as "豆瓣 (Dòubàn)". "郫县豆瓣 (Píxiàn Dòubàn)", being nationally renowned, is the must-have item in every Sichuan household and can even be found in many grocery stores overseas. Sichuan people can quickly identify a fellow-townsman by just taking out a bottle of "郫县豆瓣", and immediately use Sichuan dialect to greet, "Which

风物篇 Specialties

part of Sichuan are you from?" If just being spicy, the taste of Sichuan cuisine may not be so recognizable. Korean cuisine, Thai cuisine, Mexican cuisine and many others are all spicy in their own ways. But with Sichuan peppercorns added, the spiciness of Sichuan cuisine may be unforgettable after a taste of it. So when arriving in Sichuan, one must try dishes such as Mapo Tofu, Shuizhu Roupian (boiled pork slices in hot chili oil), Fuqi Feipian (sliced beef and ox offal in chili sauce), Spicy Chicken and so on. If one really enjoys these dishes, then congratulations! Because Sichuan is a paradise of culinary delights for lovers of the Sichuan cuisine!

However, if one finds it difficult to adapt to the Sichuan cuisine at the first try, don't worry. The new Sichuan cuisine has considered the preferences of friends from different regions and countries, emphasizing the concept of "one dish, one style; one hundred dishes, one hundred flavors". Here, "one hundred flavors" actually stand for countless flavors, which is not an exaggeration! Sichuan cuisine that people enjoy today has evolved by combining the six basic flavors of numbing, spicy, sweet, salty, sour, and bitter, creating a wide variety of taste profiles. If one is not ready for numbing and spicy food just yet, there's no problem at all. There are various other dishes instead, including Kung Pao Chicken, Shredded Pork with Fish Flavor, Sweet and Sour Ribs, Sweet Crispy Duck, and so on. In a word, once stepping into a Sichuan restaurant, one will never be disappointed!

Last but not least, the snacks in Sichuan. "川北凉粉 (Chuān běi Liángfěn)", a cold legume dish consisting of starch jelly with

第二眼看四川

向世界讲述四川故事
Second Glance at Sichuan: Telling Sichuan Stories to the World

a spicy and refreshing taste, is definitely people's go-to choice in hot summer. While in cold winter, one can savor a bowl of Mianzhu Lamb Rice Noodle or Feichangfen (mung bean noodle with pig's intestines) to warm up both the body and the soul. If one is looking for an afternoon snack, a bowl of Dan Dan Noodles is just perfect. People who have a sweet tooth will be faced with the delightful dilemma of choosing among Lai Tang Yuan (glutinous rice balls in sweet soup), Ding Ding Candy, and Sandapao. And if enjoying bold and adventurous flavors, one must try specialty dishes like Strange Flavored Rabbit Head or Leshan Bobo Chicken.

There's a story that goes, a foreign friend planned to taste all the Chinese cuisines within three months, however, three years have passed, yet he is still in Sichuan! Of course, this is only an online joke, just for fun. But the reality may be that after three years, he has not even stepped outside Chengdu!

Notes

1. 只要拿出"郫县豆瓣"，四川人便能迅速辨认出老乡。

　　In this case, "便" is an adverb used together with "如果，只要，既然", indicating the fact above must lead to the result or conclusion below. For example:

　　如果你来参加，他便也会来。
　　只要肯努力，便能成功。
　　既然大家不同意，便不要太勉强。

2. 新式川菜已经考虑过来自不同国家、不同地区朋友们的口味。

　　"考虑" is a verb which means "to think over, to consider". For example:
　　我会认真考虑这个问题，然后回答你。
　　我们不能只考虑经济，不考虑环境。

风物篇
Specialties

Questions

1. What is the most distinctive flavor of the Sichuan cuisine? Have you ever tried it? Can you get used to it?

2. Some people say that the unique cuisine of each region is always related to the local geographical environment. Do you think the spicy Sichuan cuisine is also related to the natural environment?

Discussion

It is so hard for some foreigners to accept that Sichuan people eat rabbit meat and even heads. What is your take on that?

Experience

What does "mapo" mean in the dish name "Mapo Tofu"? Why does the word "夫妻(fūqī)" (literally means "husband and wife") appear in the dish name "Fuqi Feipian (sliced beef and ox offal in chili sauce)"? Please go to a Sichuan restaurant to taste them out and find the answers. Or you can explore some dish names that interest you and try to understand their meanings.

（四）一口锅，一个江湖——火锅

火锅并不是四川人首先发明的，中国很多地方都有自己的特色火锅，例如北京的涮羊肉、广东的"打边炉"。不过，是四川人真正把"麻辣火锅"推向了全国甚至海外。现在在中国，人们一说起火锅，不特别说明，一般指的是四川的麻辣火锅。而在四川，人们对火锅的热爱更是无法用语言来形容。那么火锅的魅力到底是什么？

一是价格亲民。据说从一开始，四川火锅就是一种特别平民

第二眼看：
向世界讲述四川故事
Second Glance at Sichuan: Telling Sichuan Stories to the World

化的食物。人们把一些很便宜的菜和肉加上辣椒、花椒一起煮，既能吃饱，又能去寒湿。所以火锅就在四川慢慢流行开来了。现在，火锅仍然是大众消费的食物。一般的火锅店不会很豪华，价格很合理，特别适合家人或朋友在一起的时候吃。

二是非常热闹。吃火锅一定是很多人围坐在一起，边煮边烫，边吃边聊。这应该是吃火锅最开心的时候了，正如古代有位诗人写的"围炉聚炊欢呼处，百味消融小釜中"，意思是大家热热闹闹吃着火锅，各种味道、各种感情都在这口锅里了！所以我们说，一口锅，一个江湖。很多年前，曾经从香港传入一种"个人火锅"，但是很快就消失了。因为在很多四川人看来，一个人吃火锅，该是一件多么孤独和难过的事情啊。

三是味道刺激。四川火锅的主流是麻辣，味道非常刺激，常常吃得人眼泪和汗水一起流下来。四川人常说，"世界上没有一件难事是一顿火锅解决不了的，如果有，那就吃两顿吧！"这句话是开玩笑，却说出了真理：吃火锅可以让你心情变好。在潮湿阴冷的冬季，好朋友们一起吃火锅，既温暖了身体，也温暖了心；在闷热烦躁的夏天，边吃火锅边感觉出汗，好不畅快！遇到不顺心的事情，热热闹闹一顿火锅，就什么都忘了，明天又是新的开始。就算不吃辣也没关系，可以点上一口"鸳鸯锅"或是"锅中锅"。名字不同，但是重点都一样，就是为不吃辣的朋友准备的清汤（就是不辣的汤）火锅。于是大家在往火锅里放菜的时候，常常会说，"把这个菜放点在清汤，小明不吃辣的"。朋友之间的关心一下子就表现出来了。

风物篇
Specialties

鸳鸯锅

实际上,什么菜放红汤(就是麻辣汤)、什么菜放清汤、什么时候放什么菜都是很大的学问。再加上大家还要自己调蘸碟,菜下到锅里后要及时互相帮忙夹起来,还要抓紧时间碰杯喝酒聊天……火锅其实是把厨房和餐厅都合并到一起了。这时,我们就能看到谁是最会照顾大家的人,谁是最善于指挥的人。四川人常说,要找对象,先吃火锅。对象就是指想要谈恋爱的人,遇到很会吃火锅的人,记得赶紧表白哦。

语言点例释

1. 因为在很多四川人看来,一个人吃火锅,该是一件多么孤独和难过的事情啊。

"孤独"是一个形容词,意思是"独自一个,孤单寂寞",例如"孩子不在家的时候,他感到很孤独"。

2. 就算不吃辣也没关系,可以点上一口"鸳鸯锅"或是"锅中锅"。

"就算/就是……也……"表示让步,前一分句提出一个不太可能出现的极端情况,表示在这种情况下结果也不会改变,例如"就算成绩最好的同学也无法回答这个问题";"就是你想马上瘦下来,也不能每天不吃饭"。

第二眼看 ：
向世界讲述四川故事
Second Glance at Sichuan: Telling Sichuan Stories to the World

读后思考

1. 你吃过火锅吗？你觉得火锅的魅力在哪里？
2. 为什么四川人常说，要找对象先吃火锅？

交流讨论

有人说火锅最能体现四川人的文化性格，结合文中提到的火锅的三点魅力，和同伴谈一谈你对此是如何理解的。

(4) Hot Pot: One Pot, One World

Hot pot, also known as "火锅 (huǒguō)" in Chinese, was not originally invented in Sichuan. Many places in China have their own distinctive hot pot styles, such as Beijing's "涮羊肉 (shuàn yángròu)", a hot pot with thinly sliced lamb, and Guangdong's "打边炉 (dǎ biānlú)", literally meaning sitting and eating aside a hot pot. But the Sichuan people have truly popularized their spicy hot pot, or "麻辣火锅 (málà huǒguō)" in Chinese, across the whole country and even overseas. Now in China, when people talk about hot pot without specifying, they usually refer to the Sichuan spicy hot pot. In Sichuan, people's love for hot pot is beyond description. So, what makes hot pot so appealing?

Firstly, it is affordable. It is said that in the very past, Sichuan hot pot was a food for ordinary people. People put some inexpensive greens and meat together with chili and Sichuan peppercorns, which created a filling meal and helped ward off the coldness and dampness. As a result, hot pot gradually became popular in Sichuan, and moreover, it is still an affordable dining option for the general public today. Hot pot restaurants

风物篇
Specialties

are typically featured with very reasonable prices, neither luxurious nor extravagant, making it ideal for gatherings with family or friends.

Secondly, hot pot dining is known for its lively atmosphere. It is a gathering of family and friends, sitting around a pot, cooking and eating while chatting. This is the happiest moment when enjoying a hot pot, as a poet from ancient times described it: "gathering around the stove, joyful celebrations, a variety of flavors in the small pot", which means that everyone is enjoying the hot pot, and all kinds of flavors and emotions are mixed in that pot. Hence, people say that one hot pot creates one world. Many years ago, there was a trend of an individual hot pot style introduced from Hong Kong but disappeared soon. Because in the eyes of many Sichuan people, what a lonely and sad experience of eating hot pot alone!

Thirdly, hot pot offers a stimulating flavor experience. The mainstream flavor of Sichuan hot pot is "麻辣 (málà)", which is highly numbing and spicy, often causing tears and sweat. People in Sichuan often say, "There is not single problem in the world that cannot be solved by a hot pot meal. But if there is, then let's have two!" This humorous statement actually speaks the truth: hot pot can uplift one's mood. In a damp and cold winter, gathering with good friends to eat a hot pot meal warms up both the body and the heart. In a hot and sultry summer, sweating while eating hot pot brings a sense of refreshment. When faced with unpleasant situations, a lively hot pot session makes one forget everything, and tomorrow becomes a fresh start. Even if one doesn't want to eat spicy food, a "Yuanyang Pot" (a double-flavored pot) or a "Pot in Pot" can be opted for. The names may vary, but the focus is the same—to provide a clear broth (non-spicy soup) for those who don't eat spicy food. So, when putting vegetables into the hot pot, it is common for Sichuan people to say, "Put it in the clear broth for Xiaoming who doesn't eat spicy." It shows the care and consideration among friends.

In fact, there is a lot of skills involved in determining which ingredients should be cooked in the spicy broth and which ones should be cooked in the clear broth, as well as when to add them. In addition, people need to customize their own dipping sauces, help each other to retrieve and serve food from the pot in a timely manner, while wasting no time in drinking and chatting. Hot pot actually combines the kitchen and the dining room, from which, it can be observed that who takes the best care of everyone and who is skilled at directing the proceedings. Sichuan people often say that when looking for a boyfriend/girlfriend, it's important to first have a hot pot meal together. So, if one comes across someone who is adept at enjoying hot pot, it's a good idea to express the feelings to that person promptly.

风物篇
Specialties

Notes

1. 因为在很多四川人看来，一个人吃火锅，该是一件多么孤独和难过的事情啊。

"孤独" is an adjective which means "alone, lonely, solitary". For example:
孩子不在家的时候，他感到很孤独。

2. 就算不吃辣也没关系，可以点上一口"鸳鸯锅"或是"锅中锅"。

"就算 / 就是……也……" indicates concessive relation, in which the first clause raises an extreme situation but the second clause indicates that the result will always remain the same. For example:
就算成绩最好的同学也无法回答这个问题。
就是你想马上瘦下来，也不能每天不吃饭。

Questions

1. Have you ever tried hot pot? What do you think is the charm of it?

2. Why do Sichuan people often say that when looking for boyfriend/girlfriend, it's important to first have a hot pot meal together?

Discussion

Some people say that hot pot can best reflect the cultural character of the Sichuan people. Combining the three charms of hot pot mentioned in the text, please discuss how you understand this with others.

· 201 ·

八、艺术篇

艺术是世界共通的语言。本篇为你讲述四川人是如何用自己独创的艺术与世界对话的。

8. Art

Art is a universal language that transcends borders. This chapter represents how the Sichuan people engage in a dialogue with the world through their unique artistic creations.

第二眼看：
向世界讲述四川故事
Second Glance at Sichuan: Telling Sichuan Stories to the World

（一）可不只是"变脸"——川剧

大家一定都知道京剧吧？京剧一般翻译成"Beijing Opera"，而四川也有自己的opera，叫作川剧。别看京剧在全世界都很有名，在四川，四川人可最认川剧。不只四川，川剧在重庆、贵州和云南等地方也很受欢迎。一提起川剧，很多外国朋友都会说：知道知道，就是变脸！没错，变脸这种技艺是现在川剧表演中最具代表性的一个部分了。

变脸有好几种方法。比较常见的是利用面具来变脸。演员会把面具一层一层贴到脸上，每层面具下面都系着一条线，这条线的另一端系在腰带上。表演时，演员根据需要把面具拉下来，露出下面一层面具。听上去很简单吧？但做起来其实很困难。首先，面具是用丝绸做成的，很薄，多的时候要把七八张面具粘在一起，技艺不精的话，要么一时拉不下来，要么全部都拉了下来；其次，演员是不能让观众看到自己拉面具这个动作的，所以要一边拉，一边做出其他的舞蹈动作，而且动作一定要干脆又巧妙，才能"骗"过观众。

但是变脸可不是随便变的，必须符合川剧内容表演的需要。例如故事里的人物突然很生气，那么就要拉下蓝色的面具，生气之后又变得很忧伤，那么就要拉下白色的面具。现在有些表演把变脸单独拿出来展示，其实就不再是完整的川剧表演了，而更多是类似于杂耍之类的。所以刚开始看也许很热闹，但是看过两次，可能就会觉得没意思。

变脸时演员用到的面具上的那些图案，叫作脸谱。不用变脸的演员也会在自己脸上事先画上脸谱。充满个性和变化的脸谱是

艺术篇
Art

川剧的一大特点。我们知道京剧也有脸谱，但是川剧的脸谱相比京剧有很多独特之处。例如用动物图案表现人物特征，如有个人物的外号叫"玉蝴蝶"，于是他的脸谱上就画了一只白色的蝴蝶；再如，有个人物是蛇变的，那么他的脸谱上就有一条蓝绿色的蛇。特别有趣的是，这些动物图案要和演员的脸相配合。例如，蛇的头画在演员的嘴部，蛇身在脸上，蛇尾就在眉毛附近。这样演员张嘴，便是蛇张嘴，而脸上肌肉的运动又正好表现了蛇身的爬动。当然，同变脸一样，脸谱的颜色和图案也不仅仅是为了好看，更是为了表现剧中人物的性格、年龄的变化等。例如，红色的脸谱常常代表忠义，白色则表示狡猾。

说了那么多，我们不妨看一段川剧来"眼见为实"。不过在去之前，要了解观看的礼貌，那就是看到精彩处一定要大声喝彩！注意，表演过程中不是安静地观看，而是要不断地大声喝彩，嘴里要说"好"，手上要鼓掌，而大笑更是对演员最好的赞赏！同时，一边吃零食，一边喝茶，不时和朋友交换对故事的看法也是可以的，总之，开心享受就好。不拘泥于细节，开心就好——这也是四川文化最大的亮点之一呢！

语言点例释

1. 当然，同变脸一样，脸谱的颜色和图案也不仅仅是为了好看，更是为了表现剧中人物的性格、年龄的变化等。例如，红色的脸谱常常代表忠义，白色则代表狡猾。

　　"同"表示引起比较的事物，和"跟"的意思相近。例如"同你一样，我也是学生"。

2. 不过在去之前，要了解观看的礼貌，那就是看到精彩处一定要大声喝彩！

　　"喝彩"的意思是"大声叫好"，例如"全场观众都喝起彩来"。

· 205 ·

第二眼看四川：
向世界讲述四川故事
Second Glance at Sichuan: Telling Sichuan Stories to the World

> **拓展阅读**
>
> 杂耍
>
> 　　杂耍是中国人传统上对曲艺、杂技等技艺的合称。一般指某些活动性的游戏，如文中提到的变脸，还有民间杂耍表演木偶、魔术、猴戏等。

读后思考

1. 川剧中为什么会设计"变脸"这一环节？仅仅是为了有趣吗？

2. 观看川剧时要注意哪些礼貌？

亲身体验

在成都，有很多地方都能欣赏到优秀的川剧表演，例如蜀风雅韵川剧院。请你去这些地方或是在网上欣赏一段川剧，谈一谈自己的观感。

(1) Sichuan Opera: More than Face-Changing

　　Undoubtedly, everyone is familiar with "京剧 (Jīngjù)" in Chinese, or Beijing Opera. Well, Sichuan also has its own opera called Sichuan Opera, or "川剧 (Chuānjù)" in Chinese. No matter how popular Beijing Opera is throughout the world, Sichuan Opera always remains as the only one accepted by the local people. Actually, Sichuan Opera is not limited to Sichuan alone, as it is also popular in Chongqing, Guizhou, Yunnan and many other regions. When it comes to Sichuan Opera, lots of foreigners must say, "Yeah, I know that! The face-changing!" Yes, it is true that face-changing, the unique technique, is indeed one of the most representative parts of Sichuan Opera performances nowadays.

There are several ways to accomplish face-changing. The most common technique is to make use of masks. The artists wear layers of masks, with each layer attached to a thread that is connected to a waist belt. When performing, artists can pull down the top mask to reveal the layer underneath as needed. It sounds easy, right? But in reality, it is quite challenging. First, the masks are made of thin silk, and sometimes multiple masks are glued together, making it difficult to pull down just one layer without pulling down the entire stack. Second, the artists can't let the audience see them doing this, so they have to dance skillfully at the same time to distract the audience. Indeed, face-changing is not done randomly, which must serve the purpose of the Sichuan Opera performance. For example, if a character in the story suddenly gets angry, the artist should pull down a blue mask. Afterward, if the character transitions into a state of sadness, a white mask should be pulled down. However, it is important to note that some performances have separated face-changing from the essence of Sichuan Opera, making it more like a variety show or acrobatics. It may initially appear entertaining, however, seeing it several times can make it repetitive and boring.

The patterns on the masks used by artists during face-changing are called "Lianpu", or "脸谱 (liǎnpǔ)" in Chinese. Even the artists who do not perform face-changing still need to paint Lianpu on their faces prior to the performance. Lianpu, characterized by its uniqueness and versatility, is a distinctive feature of Sichuan Opera. While both Beijing Opera and Sichuan Opera utilize facial masks, Sichuan Opera's Lianpu has its own remarkable characteristics. For instance, animal patterns

are used to depict certain character traits. A character nicknamed "Jade Butterfly" always has a white butterfly on his mask. Similarly, a blue-green snake on the mask indicates the person was transformed from a snake. Interestingly, these animal patterns are designed to align with the artists' facial features. For example, the snake's head should be painted on the artist's mouth, the body on his face, and the tail around his eyebrows. When the artist opens his mouth, it appears as if the snake is also opening its mouth, and the movements of the facial muscles mimic the slithering of the snake. Just like the face-changing, the colors and patterns of Lianpu serve a purpose beyond aesthetics. They convey the personalities and character development of the theatrical roles. For example, red ones often represent loyal and righteous characters, while white ones indicate cunning and slyness.

Seeing is believing. It would be better for one to go and watch a live show on their own. But before going, one should pay attention to the etiquette while watching the opera, that is, to cheer up for the wonderful moments and highlights. Instead of just sitting there silently, one is expected to clap and say "Hao (Bravo)" as loud as possible. This is, considered by the Chinese people, the best praise for the performers. In addition, enjoying snacks and tea while chatting with friends is also a good choice. In a word, just enjoying oneself! Don't mind the trivial formalities, happiest is the key. The whole-hearted enjoyment is also considered as one of the most outstanding features of the Sichuan culture.

艺术篇
Art

❦ Notes ❧

1. 当然，同变脸一样，脸谱的颜色和图案也不仅仅是为了好看，更是为了表现剧中人物的性格、年龄的发展等。例如红色的脸谱常常代表忠义，白色则代表狡猾。

"同" means something that causes comparison and is similar to "跟" in meaning. For example:

同你一样，我也是学生。

2. 不过在去之前，要了解观看的礼貌，那就是看到精彩处一定要大声喝彩！

"喝彩" means "to cheer and clap". For example:

全场观众都喝起彩来。

❦ Extensive Reading ❧

Chinese Acrobatics

Chinese Acrobatics, or "杂耍 (záshuǎ)" in Chinese tradition, was a collective term for various performing arts and acrobatic skills in ancient China. It generally refers to certain interactive games and activities, such as the face-changing mentioned in the text, as well as folk juggling performances, puppetry, magic, and monkey shows.

❦ Questions ❧

1. Why is face-changing an indispensable part of Sichuan Opera? Is that just for fun?

2. What etiquette should be observed when watching Sichuan Opera?

❦ Experience ❧

In Chengdu, there are many places where you can enjoy excellent Sichuan Opera performances, such as Shufengyayun Sichuan Opera House. It is highly recommended to visit these places or watch some Sichuan Opera online, and then share your impressions with one another.

第二眼看四川：
向世界讲述四川故事
Second Glance at Sichuan: Telling Sichuan Stories to the World

（二）可不只是画画——绵竹年画

你也许没有听说过年画，但是一定听过中国人"过年"对吗？没错，年画跟过年有很紧密的关系。年画最开始就是过年时，中国人用来贴在门上的一种画。不过，这种画后来慢慢发展成一种民间艺术，是中国画中很重要的一种。中国有很多地方都以生产年画出名，四川也有好几个。绵竹年画就是最著名的一种年画。

绵竹是四川的一个城市。绵竹年画又称绵竹木版年画，就是先做好一个木版，然后在上面涂上颜色，再用一张张纸去印下来。因为绵竹市有很好的竹子做的纸，所以年画的制作材料特别好，质量也特别好。绵竹年画被称为"中国四大年画"之一，流行于整个西南地区。年画可不只是一张画那么简单，从绵竹年画的起源和发展，我们可以得知中国文化中很多有趣的知识。

第一是色彩。绵竹年画有一个与众不同的地方，就是只用木版印刷图案的轮廓，而图案上的各种颜色都是画家们用手工填上去的。所以不同画家的作品有不同的风格和趣味。总的来说，这些颜色多半是鲜艳的黄色、红色、蓝色等，给人以强烈单纯的感觉，代表了中国传统的民间审美。现在在中国还经常能看到这种颜色的组合，有的人说很俗气，有的人说有点土，但是日常生活单调而无聊，明快的颜色能给人幸福的感觉，不是很好吗？

第二是图案。绵竹年画的图案讲究对称。对称是什么意思呢？简单地说，就是左边和右边要一样，至少是基本上一样。中国传统审美就特别喜欢对称，例如北京故宫的房子都是对称修建的，看起来特别整齐，有气势。

第三是内容。年画表现得最多的是门神。古代中国人相信，如果将一些著名将军的画像贴在门上，这些将军就会像保护国家

一样保护自己的家。这些将军就叫门神。我们可以看到，大部分的门神都长得很凶恶，眼睛突出来，让人看了就害怕。但这种凶恶都是对外的，对自己的家则意味着安全。

除了门神，年画的图案还有很多，例如一些文学和戏曲故事中的人物、动物。可见在古代，文学在中国民间有相当大的影响力，成为人们生活中很重要的一个部分。

现在每年1月2日，在绵竹都会举办"绵竹年画节"。这时来自全国各地甚至海外的人们会来到"中国绵竹年画村"购买年画。当代的年画表现形式更丰富，很符合平时生活的需要，例如将传统年画的图案使用在文具、餐具或是装饰品上面，让平淡的生活变得可爱和充满乐趣。其实这也就是年画的价值，给老百姓的生活增加"色彩"。

语言点例释

1. 总的来说，这些颜色多半是鲜艳的黄色、红色、蓝色等，给人以强烈单纯的感觉，代表了中国传统的民间审美。

"总的来说"意思是"总括起来说"，意思与"总而言之、总之"相近。例如"总的来说，他的身体状态还算不错"。

2. 但这种凶恶都是对外的，对自己的家则意味着安全。

"意味着"表示含有某种意思。例如"医生的话意味着爸爸的病没有大问题"。

读后思考

1. 绵竹年画在色彩方面的特色是什么？
2. 绵竹年画的图案主要是哪些内容？

交流讨论

中国人在审美方面很讲究对称，例如绵竹年画。你还能举出哪些例子？在你的国家有类似的风格吗？

Second Glance at Sichuan: Telling Sichuan Stories to the World

请到绵竹或者网上找一找绵竹年画，感受一下年画的色彩、内容等。

(2) Mianzhu New Year Prints: More than Pictures

Though one may not have heard of New Year pictures, they must be familiar with the Chinese tradition of celebrating the Chinese New Year, right? Well, New Year pictures are closely associated with this festive occasion. Initially, they were used as decorative prints hung on doors during the Chinese New Year. However, over time, New Year pictures evolved into a popular form of folk art and became an important genre of traditional Chinese painting. Many regions in China are known for producing New Year pictures, and Mianzhu New Year Prints are among the most famous ones in Sichuan province.

Mianzhu is a city in Sichuan, and Mianzhu New Year Prints, also known as Mianzhu New Year Woodblock Prints, are created by first carving a woodblock. And then, the block is inked and used to print onto individual sheets of paper. Mianzhu is known for its high-quality bamboo paper, which makes the materials for creating New Year pictures particularly good and guarantees their excellent quality. Mianzhu New Year Prints ranks among the top four New Year Picture of China, being very popular in the southwest region of the country. New Year pictures are not merely simple paintings, however, from their origins and development, they hold a wealth of interesting knowledge

about Chinese culture.

First, the colors. Different from other New Year pictures, one unique aspect of the Mianzhu New Year Prints is that only the outlines of the patterns are printed using woodblocks, while the various colors are meticulously hand-painted by the artists later on. Thus, the pictures vary in style according to the interest of different artists. In general, the majority of those colors are vibrant and bright including yellow, red, and blue, which are strong and pure, representing the traditional folk aesthetics of China. Nowadays it is common for some people to dismiss such color combinations as gaudy or out-of-date, but in the boring and dull everyday life, such bright colors can certainly evoke one's feelings of happiness, and isn't that just wonderful?

Second, the patterns. The Mianzhu New Year Prints strives for symmetrical compositions. Simply speaking, "symmetry" means that the patterns on both sides need to be exactly the same, or at least nearly the same. The traditional Chinese aesthetics lays great emphasis on symmetry. For example, such as the Forbidden City in Beijing was also constructed with symmetrical designs, creating a neat and imposing appearance.

Third, the content. The most common theme depicted in New Years pictures is the Door Gods. The ancient Chinese people believed that if they put those portraits of well-known generals on the door, the generals would protect their homes just like protecting the country. The generals are known as the Door Gods. Most of the Door Gods are portrayed as ferocious and scaring with prominent eyes. But such fierceness is just towards the invaders, while signifying protection and safety for one's own home.

In addition to the Door Gods, there are also many other themes, such as characters and animals from certain literary works or Chinese operas. This shows that literature, in ancient China, had been quite influential and stayed a very significant part of people's lives.

Currently, there is an annual "New Year Picture Festival" in Mianzhu, which is held on January 2nd. On this day, people from all over China and even overseas come to the "Village of Mianzhu New Year Prints" to purchase the pictures. And the contemporary New Year pictures have diversified in their artistic expression, catering to the everyday needs. For example, the designs of traditional New Year pictures are used in stationery, tableware, or decorations, adding charm and fun to ordinary life. In fact, this also highlights the value of New Year pictures in bringing color to the lives of ordinary people.

Notes

1. 总的来说，这些颜色多半是鲜艳的黄色、红色、蓝色等，给人以强烈单纯的感觉，代表了中国传统的民间审美。

"总的来说" means "generally speaking", which is similar to "总而言之，总之". For example:

总的来说，他的身体状态还算不错。

2. 但这种凶恶都是对外的，对自己的家只意味着安全。

"意味着" means "to mean, to have a certain meaning". For example:

医生的话意味着爸爸的病没有大问题。

Questions

1. What are the distinctive characteristics of the Mianzhu New

Year Prints in the aspect of color?

2. What are the main themes or contents depicted in the Mianzhu New Year Prints?

Discussion

Chinese aesthetics values symmetry, as seen in Mianzhu New Year Prints. Can you provide examples from your home country with a similar style?

Experience

Please go to Mianzhu or search online for Mianzhu New Year Prints to appreciate their colors, themes, and more.

（三）可不只是唱歌——四川清音

因为普通话是中国的通用语言，所以中国大部分歌曲都是用普通话演唱的，很多四川民歌也是一样，可能用了四川民歌的曲子，但是演唱的时候还是用普通话的发音。但是还有一种民歌，历来只用四川话来唱，而且很聪明地把四川话的一些发音特点也放到了演唱中，让人听了觉得既好听，又特别。这种民歌就是"四川清音"。

四川清音最早叫作"唱小曲"或者"唱小调"。这个名字是不是很接地气？其实四川清音最早是在茶馆里面演唱的，是老百姓喜欢的音乐。要知道在20世纪30年代，四川清音可是四川地区最红的流行歌曲。当时的人说起成都的繁华就会讲"吹弹夜夜乱如麻"[1]。这里的吹弹就是四川清音，这句话的意思是走在每

---

[1] 参见清代诗人吴好山的《成都竹枝词》："名都真个极繁华，不仅炊烟廿万家。四百余条街整饬，吹弹夜夜乱如麻。"

第二眼看四川：
向世界讲述四川故事
Second Glance at Sichuan: Telling Sichuan Stories to the World

条街都能听到四川清音。

那时候，四川清音的表演形式也很简单，就是在屋子里放几张大桌子，歌手就面对观众坐着演唱。表演的时候，歌手一边唱，一边用右手敲竹鼓，左手敲檀板，来控制演唱的节奏和速度。四川清音的歌手一般都是女性，她的身后还站着一个乐队，有弹琵琶的人、弹月琴的人、拉二胡的人等。乐队有时还会为歌手伴唱。是不是有点像现代的演唱会？

四川清音的音乐非常丰富，现在保留下来的大概有100多首曲子。这些曲子有的来自四川民歌，有的来自四川扬琴曲，还有的来自其他地区的民歌。四川清音把这些不同风格的音乐加工，然后再以自己特有的方式演唱出来，其中最有特色的就是"哈哈腔"。哈哈腔是一种演唱技巧，就是歌手在演唱时会发出好像"哈哈"的笑音，能够很好地调动观众的情绪。这种技巧有点像美声唱法中的花腔，意大利语叫 coloratura。

现在的四川清音表演有了很多创新。歌手一般都是站着演唱，而且有时不只有一个歌手，还有两个人的对唱和更多人的合唱等形式，这样演员可以有更多的动作，还能互相配合，表演形式更加活泼。

但是和很多非物质文化遗产一样，在当代，四川清音也不流行了。很多四川的年轻人甚至都没有听说过四川清音。我们这一篇讲到的川剧、年画、传统舞蹈等非物质文化遗产其实都面临类似的问题：大家都说好，但是既不了解，也不懂怎样欣赏，特别是年轻人，离传统好像越来越远了。这个问题的出现有多方面的原因，或是因为现代生活的环境变了，例如一些少数民族地区也已经成为城市，人们似乎没有机会再跳传统的舞蹈；或是因为现

代人的审美变了,例如川剧的表演比较程式化,而现代人可能更喜欢追求变化;或是某些外来文化有更发达的传播技术,比较强势,让年轻人产生自己本土的文化已经过时的错觉……不过,现在中国人已经越来越重视传统文化传承的问题,政府也设立了很多项目进行保护,例如建立"非物质文化遗产数字博物馆",再如帮助艺术家们继续传统艺术的工作,等等。

语言点例释

1. 哈哈腔是一种演唱技巧,就是歌手在演唱时会发出好像"哈哈"的笑音,能够很好地调动观众的情绪。

"调动"的意思是"使……发挥积极性",例如"要注意调动孩子的学习兴趣"。

2. 这个问题的出现有多方面的原因,或是因为现代生活的环境变了,例如一些少数民族地区也已经成为城市,人们似乎没有机会再跳传统的舞蹈;或是因为现代人的审美变了,例如川剧的表演比较程式化,而现代人可能更喜欢追求变化;或是某些外来文化有更发达的传播技术,比较强势,让年轻人产生了自己本土的文化已经过时的错觉……

"或是……,或是……"表示选择,例如"这件事情或是哥哥做的,或是弟弟做的"。

延伸阅读

非物质文化遗产

非物质文化遗产是指一些优秀传统文化的表现形式,以及与传统文化表现形式相关的实物和场所。"艺术篇"中提到的四种艺术都是中国国家级的非物质文化遗产。

读后思考

1. 四川清音在发音方面有什么特色?

2. 根据你的经验,非物质文化遗产在当代的传承遇到了哪些困难?

Second Glance at Sichuan: Telling Sichuan Stories to the World

交流讨论

像清音这样的传统艺术似乎离当代年轻人越来越远。在你看来，有哪些方法可以帮助传统艺术吸引更多的年轻人参与呢？

亲身体验

请利用网上资源观看一段清音表演，感受一下"哈哈腔"。

(3) Sichuan Qingyin: More than Singing

Putonghua, the standard Chinese, is the official language of China, therefore, most Chinese songs are sung in Putonghua. So are many Sichuan folk songs, which keep the distinctive melodies but use the pronunciation of Putonghua. Nonetheless, there is a type of folk song that has always been sung in Sichuan dialect, cleverly incorporating the pronunciation characteristics of Sichuan dialect into the singing, which makes it both pleasant to hear and unique. This type of folk song is called "Sichuan Qingyin".

Sichuan Qingyin was initially called "唱小曲 (chàng xiǎoqǔ)" or "唱小调 (chàng xiǎodiào)", which literally means "singing minor tunes". Doesn't the name sound down-to-earth? In fact, Sichuan Qingyin was first performed in tea houses and was people's favorite music. In the 1930s, it was the most popular genre of music in Sichuan area. To describe the prosperity of Chengdu, people used to say, "with the sounds of flutes and strings springy and busy like tangled threads

every night"[1]. Here "the sounds of flutes and strings" refer to Sichuan Qingyin, and the cited line means that one can hear Sichuan Qingyin across every street every night.

During that time, the performance style of Sichuan Qingyin was very simple: the singer, sitting in a room with several big tables, facing the audience and singing to them. While singing, the singer would strike the bamboo drum with the right hand and play hardwood clappers with the left hand, in order to control the rhythm and speed of the performance. Usually, the singers of Sichuan Qingyin were female, with a band behind consisting of musicians playing instruments such as the *pipa*, *yueqin*, *erhu* and other instruments. Sometimes, the band would also provide the accompaniment for the singer. Doesn't it sound a bit like the today's concert?

Sichuan Qingyin has a rich repertoire of music, with around 100 or more preserved melodies. Among them, some are derived from folk songs of Sichuan, some are from dulcimer tunes, and others are from folk songs of other regions. In other words, Sichuan Qingyin has recomposed and polished different music styles, and then performed them in its own unique way. The most distinctive singing technique is called "Haha Qiang". Just as its name implies, singers emit laughter-like sounds, effectively evoking emotions in the audience. This technique is

---

1 This line refers to the Qing Dynasty poet Wu Haoshan's "Chengdu Bamboo Branch Songs": "The renowned city is truly bustling, with smoke curling out of twenty thousand households' chimneys; Over four hundred streets and lanes are orderly arranged, with the sounds of flutes and strings springy and busy like tangled threads every night."

somewhat similar to the coloratura technique in operatic singing.

Nowadays, many innovations have been made in Sichuan Qingyin performances. Different from the past, singers generally stand while singing, and sometimes there are duets or even group choruses, allowing for more dynamic movements and coordination among the performers, which makes the performances livelier.

However, just like many other intangible cultural heritages, Sichuan Qingyin also appears less popular in modern times. Lots of young people may not have even heard of it. Frankly speaking, the intangible cultural heritages we discuss in this chapter, such as Sichuan Opera, Mianzhu New Year Prints, and traditional dances, are all faced with the similar challenge: they are highly regarded, but often not understood nor appreciated, especially by young people who seem to be moving further away from tradition. There are many reasons for this phenomenon. Some are due to changes in the modern living environment. For example, some ethnic minority areas have developed into modern cities, so people seem to have fewer opportunities to engage in traditional dances. Some are due to shifts in modern aesthetics. For instance, Sichuan Opera performances can be seen as more formalized, while modern audiences may prefer constant change and novelty. Additionally, with the spread of technologies and social media, certain foreign cultures may appear more dominant, leading young people to perceive their own culture as outdated. However, nowadays, the Chinese people are increasingly valuing the issue of preserving traditional culture, and the government has established many initiatives

艺术篇 Art

for its protection, including the establishment of the Digital Museum of Intangible Cultural Heritage, and the support for artists to continue their careers in traditional arts.

Notes

1. 哈哈腔是一种演唱技巧，就是歌手在演唱时会发出好像"哈哈"的笑音，能够很好地调动观众的情绪。

"调动" means "to mobilize (one's enthusiasm, initiative, etc.)". For example:

要注意调动孩子的学习兴趣。

2. 这个问题的出现有多方面的原因，或是因为现代生活的环境变了，例如一些少数民族地区也已经成为城市，人们似乎没有机会再跳传统的舞蹈；或是因为现代人的审美变了，例如川剧的表演比较程式化，而现代人可能更喜欢追求变化；或是某些外来文化有更发达的传播技术，比较强势，让年轻人产生了自己本土的文化已经过时的错觉……

The structure "或是……或是……" is used to list alternative possibilities. For example:

这件事情或是哥哥做的，或是弟弟做的。

Extensive Reading

Intangible Cultural Heritage

Intangible Cultural Heritage refers to the forms of outstanding traditional culture, as well as the physical objects and places associated with these forms. The four kinds of art mentioned in this chapter are all listed as the National Intangible Cultural Heritage of China.

Questions

1. What are the characteristics of Sichuan Qingyin in pronunciation?

2. Based on your experience, what are the challenges faced by intangible cultural heritage in contemporary times?

Discussion

Traditional art like Sichuan Qingyin seems to be increasingly distant from contemporary young people's lives. In your opinion, what methods can we take to help traditional art attract more young participants?

Experience

Please watch a Sichuan Qingyin performance online and appreciate the "Haha Qiang" vocal technique.

（四）可不只是一种舞蹈——四川少数民族舞蹈

舞蹈是四川传统文化和艺术中一个重要的部分。从传统舞蹈中，我们不仅能欣赏到美，还可以看到各有特色的民族生活和文化。

㑇舞是白马藏族的传统舞蹈。白马藏族的语言和文化很有特色。白马藏族现在主要生活在四川省的阿坝藏族羌族自治州，人口2万多。"㑇"是白马语的词，意思是美好的面具舞，汉语一般叫"十二相舞"。这种舞蹈最大的特点是跳舞的人都戴着各种各样的面具。大部分面具的样式是动物的头，有牛头、蛇头、鸡头、虎头等。为什么要戴这些动物头面具呢？这是因为古代的白马人相信"万物有灵"，意思是所有的东西，特别是动物，都和人一样有灵魂。所以人可以和动物一起跳舞、交流，和谐相处。在古代，㑇舞有很多功能，可以用来祭祀神灵，也可以在各种喜庆的场合表演以祝愿大家健康快乐。

与白马藏族欢快的㑇舞不同，卡斯达温舞则是一种雄壮奔放

的舞蹈。这是羌族的一种传统舞蹈。羌族与白马藏族一样,生活在四川省阿坝藏族羌族自治州。"卡斯达温"是羌语,意思是穿铠甲。什么是铠甲呢?你可能在中国的电影里看见过,在古代的战争中,也就是"冷兵器时代",军人们面对敌人的武器,要保护自己的身体就会穿上铠甲。卡斯达温舞表演中,男性舞者穿着铠甲跳舞,充满力与美。那我们来猜一猜,这种舞蹈会不会跟战争有关?没错!卡斯达温舞最早是羌族人在参加战争之前用来祭祀的一种活动。但是慢慢地,人们觉得这种舞蹈能让人受到鼓励,所以在过年、结婚或是有人去世时也会表演。表演时,15岁以上的人都必须参加,大家在一个最受尊敬的人的带领下,一边唱歌一边跳舞,男声低,女声高,配合起来,独具魅力。

  这两种舞蹈都是中国国家级的非物质文化遗产。非物质文化遗产,简单来说,就是一些特别珍贵的传统文化形式,例如艺术、体育、手工艺。这些传统文化形式是以人为中心的"活"的文化遗产,是中国人在生活中对自然、生死、天地等永恒话题的态度的表达,而这些表达对今天的我们来说是一笔巨大的精神财富。中国的非物质文化遗产保护项目对少数民族文化会特意关注。有人说,这是不是有点不公平?是不是应该按照这个文化的影响力来决定是不是很重要?但其实这就是最公平的方法,因为中华民族是由56个民族构成的,每个民族的文化都很重要,缺了谁都绝对不行。非物质文化遗产中有每个民族的语言、风俗、思想等文化要素。从某种意义上说,保护非物质文化遗产,就是在保护和传承一个民族的文化。

语言点例释

1. 在古代，伯舞有很多功能，可以用来祭祀神灵，也可以在各种喜庆的场合表演来祝愿大家健康快乐。

"祝愿"是一个动词，表示用语言对人或事表示良好的愿望。例如"衷心祝愿我们两国永远友好下去"。"祝愿"也可以是名词，表示用语言表示出来的美好愿望，例如"请接受我们的美好祝愿"。

2. 中国的非物质文化遗产保护项目对少数民族文化会特意关注。

"特意"是一个方式副词，表示某事是专门为了某一目的或者出于重视而进行的，例如"这个菜是妈妈特意为你做的，你要多吃一些"。

读后思考

1. 为什么说保护非物质文化遗产就是传承了一个民族的文化？

2. 你的民族文化中有哪些非物质文化遗产？现在得到了哪些保护？

交流讨论

中国有56个民族，除了文中提到的，你还知道哪些富有民族特色的舞蹈，请和同伴交流、分享。

亲身体验

请利用网上资源观看一段伯舞或者卡斯达温舞表演，感受一下这些艺术的特色与美妙。

(4) Folk Dances of Ethnic Minorities in Sichuan: More than Dancing

Dancing is a significant component of traditional culture and art in Sichuan. One can not only appreciate the beauty of dancing moves, but

also witness the various ethnic lifestyles and cultures.

Zhou Dance, or "伯舞 (Zhòu wǔ)" in Chinese, is the traditional dance of Baima Tibetan ethnic group. Their language and culture are highly distinctive. The Baima Tibetans primarily live in Aba Tibetan and Qiang Autonomous Prefecture in Sichuan, with a population of more than 20,000. "Zhou" is a word in Baima language, which means a splendid mask dance. It is commonly known as the "Twelve-Phase Mask Dance" in standard Chinese. The most remarkable feature of this dance is that all the dancers wear various masks, most of which represent animal heads, such as ox, snake, rooster, tiger, and etc. But why do the dancers wear those masks? The reason is that the ancient Baima people believed in "all things possess a spirit", which means all things, especially animals, have spiritual essence like humans. Thus, humans can dance and communicate with animals in harmonious coexistence. In ancient times, Zhou Dance had a lot of functions, varying from worshiping deities to wishing everyone good health and happiness on festive occasions.

Different from the joyful Zhou Dance, Kasidawen Dance of Qiang ethnic group is very grand and vigorous. Like the Baima Tibetans, the Qiang people also live in Aba Tibetan and Qiang Autonomous Prefecture in Sichuan. "Kasidawen" is a term in Qiang language, which means "wearing armor". What is "armor"? Perhaps one may have seen it in many Chinese movies. During the ancient times like in the era of "cold weapons", soldiers wore armors to protect their bodies when facing enemy's weapons. In Kasidawen Dance, male dancers

dress in battle armors to show both their strength and beauty. So, it is easy to infer that the dance is related to warfare. Indeed, it originated from a pre-war ritual. As time went by, people have realized that the dance has amazing power of encouragement and motivation even during peace times, so it has been also performed in new year events, wedding ceremonies or funerals. Anyone over 15 years old must join the show. Led by the most respected person, people sing and dance together, with low male voices and high female tones, harmonizing to create a unique charm.

Both of the dances have been regarded as China's national intangible cultural heritage which encompasses precious traditional cultural forms such as art, sports and handicrafts. These human-centered forms are "living" cultural heritage, demonstrating the attitudes of the Chinese people towards the eternal topics such as nature, life, death, and the universe. As for the modern people, these expressions are a tremendous spiritual wealth. Speaking of the intangible cultural heritage protection project in China, a special focus is given to the cultural heritage of ethnic minorities. Some may question whether this is unfair and if the importance should be determined based on the influence of a particular culture. However, this is actually the most equitable approach because China is composed of 56 ethnic groups, and the culture of each ethnic group is absolutely significant and indispensable. The intangible cultural heritage includes many cultural elements of these ethnic groups, such as languages, customs, and beliefs. In a sense, protecting intangible cultural heritage is equivalent to inheriting the culture.

Notes

1. 在古代，伫舞有很多功能，可以用来祭祀神灵，也可以在各种喜庆的场合表演来祝愿大家健康快乐。

"祝愿" is a verb, which means to use words to express good will toward someone or something. For example:

衷心祝愿我们两国永远友好下去。

"祝愿" can also be a noun, meaning good wishes. For example:

请接受我们的美好祝愿。

2. 中国的非物质文化遗产保护项目对少数民族文化会特意关注。

"特意" is an adverb that signifies an action performed deliberately for a specific purpose or with particular significance (on purpose). For example:

这个菜是妈妈特意为你做的，你要多吃一些。

Questions

1. Why is it said that protecting intangible cultural heritage is equivalent to inheriting the culture of a nation?

2. What intangible cultural heritages does your ethnic culture have? What protections are in place now?

Discussion

There are 56 ethnic groups in China. In addition to those mentioned above, do you know any other dances with unique ethnic characteristics? Please share with others.

Experience

Please watch a performance of Zhou Dance or Kasidawen Dance to learn more about the distinctive features and beauty of these art forms.

后记

对我们来说,《第二眼看四川——向世界讲述四川故事》的写作与出版是一段与朋友们携手前行的温暖旅程。

首先,感谢几位倾心投入的研究生——魏馨怡、邓亚男、李雨瞳。三位年轻的朋友不仅在本书"语言点例释""读后思考""交流讨论""亲身体验"的编撰方面做出实质性贡献,更在工作过程中持续贡献充满活力的创意,让本书的练习部分充满鲜活的细节与丰富的故事。因为有了她们,这些问答与体验活动的设计才更加贴近年轻读者,更易于被世界各地的中文学习者理解和接受。

感谢四川大学出版社的周洁老师,作为本书的责任编辑,她不仅在字句间反复打磨,更以专业的眼光帮助我们理清思路,完善结构。

还要特别感谢曾经参与四川大学海外教育学院"巴蜀文化"课程学习的同学们。正是他们在课堂上的一次次提问、讨论和热烈分享,给予了我们无数新的思考角度和感悟瞬间。他们是这本书真正的灵感源泉,也是我们讲好四川故事的最重要动力。

最后感谢所有支持和陪伴这本小书诞生的朋友们。刘克奇慷慨"赞助"了熊熊燃烧的篝火图,而其他摄影师美图[1]亦让川风

---

1 本书摄影师美图均来自 www.veer.com。

蜀韵显影眼前。因为热爱，所以讲述，希望书中的文图能够将这段旅程的温馨持续传递，让更多的中文学习者透过故事，看到一幅真实、生动、可亲可感的四川画卷。

李韵　于婧

2025 年 6 月 1 日

 **Postscript**

For us, the writing and publication of A Second Look at Sichuan: Telling Sichuan Stories to the World has been a warm journey shared hand in hand with our friends.

First and foremost, we would like to thank the devoted graduate students——WEI Xinyi, DENG Yanan, and LI Yutong. These young friends not only made substantial contributions to the sections "Notes", "Questions", "Discussion" and "Experience", but also continuously brought vibrant ideas throughout the process. Thanks to them, the exercises are filled with lively details and rich stories, making the designs of the Q&A and experiential activities resonate more deeply with young readers, and easier to understand and embrace for Chinese learners worldwide.

We are also deeply grateful to Ms.ZHOU Jie from Sichuan University Press. As the editor of this book, she not only carefully refined every word and sentence but also helped us clarify our ideas and improve the structure with her professional insight.

Special thanks go to all the students who participated in the "Bashu Culture" courses at the College of Overseas Education, Sichuan University. It was their questions, discussions, and enthusiastic sharing in class that provided us with countless new perspectives and inspiring moments. They are the true source of inspiration for this book and the most important motivation for us to tell Sichuan's stories well.

Finally, we would like to express our gratitude to all the friends who supported and accompanied the birth of this little book. LIU Keqi generously offered her stunning bonfire photo for us, while other photographers' beautiful images vividly brought the charm of Sichuan to life. It is out of love that we tell these stories, and we hope the words and images in this book can continue to share this warmth, allowing more Chinese learners to glimpse a true, lively, and endearing Sichuan through these stories.

LI Yun, YU Jing

June 1, 2025